BRICK AND MORTAR
PIGGY BANKS

*YOUR GUIDE TO CREATING
LIFE-CHANGING WEALTH THROUGH
REAL ESTATE INVESTMENT*

NICHOLAS A. DUNLAP

This book is dedicated to my dad. Not just for teaching me the real estate business, but for being my best friend and my idol. It's also for my mom, who helped me get a work permit when I was 12 and never let me sleep in. I'm responsible because of you. And to my beautiful wife, for listening and inspiring. You're my muse. I love you all.

– ND

Contents

PART I:

The Four Benefits to Investing in Real Estate

Introduction

"Little pig, little pig, let me in."
"Not by the hair on my chinny, chin, chin."

CONVERSATION BETWEEN THE BIG, BAD WOLF
AND ONE OF THREE LITTLE PIGS

We all know the tale of the three little pigs: the English fairytale that we learned as children detailing the affairs of, you guessed it—three little pigs whose lives each take different turns based on the materials used in the composition of their houses. As investors, we hope to mirror the results achieved by the last pig standing through the resilience of our investment portfolios. A diverse portfolio that stands up to inflation, provides cash flow, yields equity buildup and helps to off-set income through tax shelter is the mark of a stone fort. This also happens to be the mark of a real estate investment. And while it is important to diversify your portfolio to include all asset types— stocks, bonds and gold included—you want to anchor your portfolio with solid assets that will consistently perform and have historically outperformed the competition. Yes, I am talking about real estate.

Only in real estate have I seen individuals acquire and develop their wealth in as little as a couple of months, just to continue building their portfolio and increasing their holdings. Young people, old people, students, professionals—it is never too early or too late to invest. Perhaps one of the most comforting things about investing in real estate is its physicality, meaning that all things considered, if the investment were to stop performing financially, you would still have a physical, tangible asset that you could touch, walk around, sleep in, work on or take apart. You can't do that with stock. Bonds? Forget about it. Gold? Well, you could always make jewelry.

Outside of this physical comfort lies the amazing depth of human emotion that is created and sparked by real estate. The hospital that you were born in. The restaurant that you and your significant other dined at on your first date. Your first apartment. The office building where you got fired from your first real job. Real estate is not just an investment. It is where people create memories. And as long as there are memories to be created, real estate will be one of the soundest investments that a person can make. If you were paying attention, you realize that each type of real estate that was just mentioned is from a different segment of the commercial real estate market: multifamily (apartments), office, commercial and retail real estate, to be exact.

Multifamily investments or apartment complexes as they are more commonly known, are the property type of focus herein. Of course, if you are interested in sort of a primer in real estate investments of other property types, this book will still be of use to you. However, it will not provide the handholding that it will for soon-to-be apartment owner/operators. What's more, it is important to understand that in comparing property types, you will often see the term "commercial" or "residential". Please understand that by residential, I am talking about single family residences whereas commercial refers to apartment complexes and the like.

That's right, we will not be talking about single-family residences in this book. No, not at all. (If that's what you were hoping to learn more about when you bought the book, I hope you kept your receipt.) Instead, we will focus on the financial benefits of investing in commercial real estate, the benefits behind investing in real estate, how to structure your investment and acquisition of a piece of commercial property, and finally, how to manage your investment property or how to hire the right management company for your investment property.

One of the reasons I prefer commercial real estate to residential real estate is that one is bought and sold based on feelings, the other is traded based on numbers. By now, I hope you've guessed that commercial real estate is bought based on numbers. And once you understand the different cost and investment measures of commercial real estate, you will have a firm grasp on what will make a good investment that you should move on (and what you should pass on). Simply put, the numbers don't lie.

So whether you are a beginning investor looking for pointers as you begin your career or a seasoned investor with a number of multifamily complexes or commercial buildings in your portfolio, there is something in this book for you. There are an assortment of terms, pointers and suggestions on business strategy. Conveniently, this book is broken down into three sections that could each stand alone as its own body of work. The first portion focuses on why you should invest in real estate. The second portion focuses on how to invest in commercial real estate. And the third portion focuses on how to manage your real estate investment. We in the industry refer to this as being from "womb to tomb" or beginning to end.

Through it all, you'll see that the secret to successful investing is twofold: effective underwriting and astute management. If you follow these two simple steps and avoid the pitfalls of greed, influence and over-projection, your investment goals will come true. Always remember to stand firm in the face of greed and influence. Those two factors have decimated many a real estate portfolio. It is your money, so listen to and decide for yourself.

Woven into the lesson plan are the firsthand accounts from a dozen or so investors who have become multi-millionaires through investing in real estate. Not only will you become aware of their secrets and learn what has made them successful, you will learn of the pitfalls they wish they had avoided early on in their careers. Their losses are truly your gains.

Having grown up in the real estate business, I have the unique advantage of having been on due diligence walks with my dad on apartment buildings when I was 9 years old. My bedtime stories were of business trips and new buildings that my dad had helped someone buy or had bought himself. In fact, I remember a car ride to school when I was 12 where my dad asked me if I knew what OPM was. Other People's Money, I soon learned, was a reference to earning a financial return on borrowed funds. By my mid-20s, I had bought and sold millions of dollars in real estate. It's not all I know, but it's what I love. It's in my blood. And it would be a shame to not share this wealth of information with you. There are countless opportunities in the real estate market, and there are more than enough assets for us all to invest and live comfortably. So let's get started.

CHAPTER 1:
For Greater Results, Start Here

*"The way to get started is to quit talking
and begin doing."*

WALT DISNEY

First things first: this is not an infomercial. Erik Estrada will not sell you a timeshare. You will not learn how to purchase a house that sold for $550,000 two years ago for $99 today. This is not an audiotape that upon your first listen will make you bleed, sweat and cry money. Oh, and another thing: none of these programs, gimmicks or scams to get rich quick or overnight work. The only ways to get rich overnight (legally) that I know of are through an inheritance, the lottery or a gigantic win on an underdog bet. So, hopefully we can agree that there is a difference between making a real estate investment and building your portfolio and a quick elevator ride to wealth. It just doesn't happen that way. And one more thing: I am not selling you anything. You already bought my book and now it is up to you to study, follow and implement the strategies you learn herein. And although there are secrets to success, there are no shortcuts to success. See, it is not that these systems are flawed, it is that they are setup to appeal to your emotions so that you call at 11:30 pm, 3:00 am or 10:30 am when you SHOULD be doing a number of other things, none of which include getting fleeced by a former sit-com star or a self-proclaimed high school dropout who struck it rich by flipping houses. These are marketing systems that generate revenue for the production company and leave you with a system not worth the paper on which it's written. Not this book, though.

This is about creating your wealth through the world's oldest profession. No, not prostitution. They paid rent to someone, right? You see, wealthy cavemen did not flip caves. They owned and lived in a big cave and acquired multiple smaller caves or even hills or mountains of caves that they rented out to the cavemen who were conserving resources or had not yet started a family. Sure, that could be an exaggeration, and I don't have rock-solid evidence (pun intended), but it's something that is likely true. Full disclosure: I am not a cave man and do not claim to know more about history than I learned during my high school or undergraduate days. What I do know is that most Americans are trapped in a struggle, a struggle that lies between the frustration over one's earnings, the desire to live a greater life and the ability to create a source of passive income that will not only supplement one's income but help to bolster one's lifestyle. And if the cavemen did it, so can you.

My clients are attorneys, accountants, doctors, business owners and other professionals who have made money selling their time to generate revenue and savings that they have in turn invested into income-producing real estate. The result? Millionaire after multi-millionaire created through the solo or joint acquisition of commercial or multi-family property. Not to mention, these hourly-earning professionals much prefer the passive income stream created by their real estate holdings to the grind du jour of their 9 to 5. Unless you are a movie star, professional athlete or independently wealthy socialite, you will need a passive income stream to help you build wealth through cash flow, equity buildup and tax benefits. For the record, smart movie stars and athletes invest their money as well.

Back to the book.

This book is setup in three different sections to mirror the real estate investment process. The three steps or sections are: The Four Benefits, Due Diligence Done Right and Winning Property Management Strategies. Although you can skip around and read the book front-to-back or back-to-front, you will get the most bang for buck by reading this book just like you would read any other bit of Western literature, from front to back and from cover to cover.

We will not focus too much on market-specific details in the investment of management section. We will instead provide insight and strategy, but will suggest that you pursue and verify the legality of or ability to do what is recommended on your own. Yes, that was a waiver. Depending on where you are located within the United States, there may quite possibly be a higher barrier to entry or obstacle with regard to sales prices, deposit requirements and the availability of financing for a particular asset class. What you will learn are the fundamentals of why you should own lots of commercial real estate, how to identify solid real estate investments, the art of negotiating and acquiring real estate and how to manage your holdings or outsource the management post-acquisition.

Now, if you have been so fortunate as to inherit property or even an interest in a portfolio, we can also help. You see, in order to truly maximize your return, you must know the ins and outs, the secrets, the benefits and the tricks. We will get you up and running in no time. But remember, there is no shortcut to success, unless you are independently wealthy.

Really, the only thing between you and your investment is the right team and your down payment. If you cannot do it on your own, find a partner. The only thing between you and your success is YOU! So make it happen.

At the bare minimum of eight hours a day, five days a week, the average fully employed American is overworked, to say the least. Consider the fact that 39% of American workers are working more than 40 hours a week, and we see that free time is a rarity for most. All too often, people rely on their salary and savings as opposed to a source of passive income to aide in supporting their lifestyle and planning for retirement. Imagine that you could supplement your income by investing a portion of your current savings in a large, physical object that would provide you with periodic financial returns in monthly and/ or annual lump sums. What's more, this object could potentially serve four purposes, including: Cash Flow, Equity Buildup/Appreciation, Tax Savings and a Hedge Against Inflation. This object is commercial real estate, and the opportunities are in fact possible.

Through investing in real estate, you can take steps towards your current and future financial goals. For some, this translates to more vacation time, a nicer home, children's college funds or even personal retirement. If you don't have children or maybe you hate children, don't hate me. I am simply playing to the emotions of my reader. It's what we writers do. It has to do with identifying our audience. So, if you shake your head or cringe every time you see the word "children," insert whatever non-parental item you would like; I won't take offense.

Now, back to business. The following points will demonstrate to you the four benefits of investing in commercial real estate and help you determine the next step in your quest for financial wealth and well-being. Later, you will learn how to locate and identify these investment opportunities within the marketplace. Finally, you will learn how to care for your properties and preserve your passive income stream through the professional management of your property. If you do not already own apartments or commercial real estate, consider this book your best investment yet. The return on investment will beat the bank by a long-shot. Of course, in today's market, that's not saying much.

Tied into the facts, definitions, descriptions and details are individual accounts of how a number of wealthy real estate owners got their start and why they prefer real estate to other asset classes. While some of these individuals might be well-known, famous or otherwise household names, there are even more who are virtually unknown outside of the real estate circle within their local markets. This was done intentionally to demonstrate that all it takes is determination and know-how. With those two traits or skills, you can either raise money from investors or deploy your own capital and become successful.

This book will give you invaluable tools and resources to assist in the investment process, including a due diligence checklist, spreadsheet for use in underwriting and help putting together your real estate investment toolkit that will aide in your success. Sure, you will wish you read this book five or 10 years ago, but instead of focusing on what you should have or could have done, harness your energy into becoming successful today, becoming successful right NOW. Whether that is today, tomorrow or in the near future is entirely up to you.

CHAPTER 2:

The Four Benefits – Defined, Explained and Made Simple

"Write your injuries in dust, your benefits in marble."

BENJAMIN FRANKLIN

Although everyone has a different reason for investing, and those reasons can in turn lead to an exponential array of lifestyle benefits, there are in fact just four benefits of owning real estate as an investment. In what I feel is the most important order, they are as follows: cash flow, equity build-up, tax shelter and a hedge against inflation. While some of these are easier to interpret and understand than others, they each play an important part in real estate's role as one of the more preferred and yet often underappreciated investment vehicles.

In order to understand the four benefits, it is important to go pedestrian. That is, think entry level and start from the ground-up. Think learning to walk before you can run. You see, knowing the story behind the benefit and knowing how to explain it to someone else will help you better understand and identify the benefit yourself. It's go time. We'll start with my favorite.

Cash flow

Envision yourself reclined in a boat in a beautiful lagoon, anchored beneath what appears to be a picturesque waterfall. As you look up, you realize that flowing down from the waterfall is not crisp, clear water, but firm, green hundred dollar bills. They have begun to fill the boat, and so you must stand up with open arms to allow room for more. It's a fantastic image, is it not?

The best part is that in fact, it is true. Well, it is true in its literal sense. Cash flow is defined as the periodic disbursal of funds generated by an asset. In the metaphor, the waterfall represents a commercial property (asset), and the sea of green represents a monthly deposit or disbursal flowing from it.

Over a fiscal period of time, be it a month or year, the gross or total income is collected and from this amount, the operating expenses are paid (subtracted). The gross income less the operating expenses results in the net operating income. If you have a loan on the property, you will subtract any loan payments; if not, the figure that you are looking at is your before-tax cash flow. Yes, you will get a visual description as well. Read on.

Let's go back to the boat beneath the waterfall. Now, imagine yourself fishing beneath the waterfall with a net. After you dip your net in the water and have filled it, you have in your net the gross income. The net is overfilled, so you must shake out your net. Now, picture yourself shaking the gross income and in turn, shaking loose the operating expenses. When you pull your net out this time, you have what is in fact your net operating income. From the net operating income, the debt service (mortgage) is paid and you arrive at your before-tax cash flow. The cash flow is what you make each month or year, depending on when you choose to release funds. Cash flow is the most easily recognizable benefit of investing in commercial real estate, and it is most easily understood as the spendable proceeds or net profits at the end of an operational period.

After the bills are paid, cash flow is what is left in the bank or in your pocket. Investors who buy for cash flow are typically the least speculative as they are basing their investment and acquisition on the property's current performance with an understanding that there might be upside potential in the future. When an asset is purchased, there will be a gross income and there are expenses associated with it, thus yielding the net operating income. Unless it was purchased all cash, there will be debt service. After paying the debt service, there will be a before-tax cash flow.

Before-tax cash flow can be either positive or negative, meaning you can buy a property that is steadily producing a positive stream of income or you can purchase a property that is struggling and actually losing money on a periodic basis. If you are considering an investment with negative cash flow, ask yourself the following questions:

- Am I ready to lose money and come out of pocket to support the property in the immediate future?
- How long until the property will produce positive cash flow?
- What must I do as the owner to encourage positive cash flow?
- Is positive cash flow possible given the current financing in place?

Understanding these factors ahead of your investment will help you determine whether or not this potential acquisition is the right one for you. Investors looking to help supplement their lifestyles or perhaps put ongoing proceeds from a real estate investment into their savings or maybe even acquire additional interests in real property often choose the positive cash-flow investment. There is no such thing as a no-brainer when it comes to investing, but this is about as close as it gets.

Equity Buildup/Appreciation

Analogy-hop with me here if you would. We will go from talking about waterfalls to sandwiches. You should get hungry, so grab a snack. Now, if cash flow were the baked bread packed with condiments on your real estate investment sandwich, equity would be the meat. Appreciation in your asset's value will result in an increase your equity, creating opportunities to leverage a particular asset into multiple properties through the use of this appreciate value. Now, back to the sandwich. Sort of like the cash-flowing waterfall that we just detailed, this sandwich will also require a bit of imagination.

Picture yourself at a New York deli, reviewing a picture-packed menu of delicious sandwiches.

You decide on the roast beef. The sandwich arrives, and you choose to attack the pickles first. You look on in amazement at the mountain of meat that sits on your plate. You snap into a pickle when all of a sudden, the meat on your sandwich appears to have increased. Wait, now you finish the pickle and you see that the meat has doubled!

You did nothing to the sandwich. No waiter or busboy delivered extras and for some reason, you have double the meat on your sandwich. In the time it took for you to eat a few pickles and slurp down your Coke, the amount of meat on your sandwich has doubled. And the best part, you did nothing more than let it sit on your plate.

Holding commercial real estate over an extended period of time is a lot like the magically growing roast beef sandwich depicted herein. Regardless of your point of entry into the market, real estate is cyclical and values will rise or appreciate over time, ultimately resulting in the buildup and increase of equity in your investment. And no, I would not encourage you to eat a roast beef sandwich that mysteriously grows or multiplies in size. But I will encourage you to invest in real estate because this is exactly what happens over an extended period of time.

Yes, that's right…

Equity buildup is the benefit of ownership most closely associated with the holding of property over time. Timing is essential in a business so closely associated with peaks and valleys. The real estate market is no different than any other market or economy in that it is cyclical in nature and yields circumstances where one entry point is better than others and can not only have a significant impact on the overall profitability of your investment, but on the ability to improve your equity position.

It is often said that you make your money in real estate at the point of purchase; thus, it is important to be fully aware of the market's performance upon making your acquisition. Understand where you are within the real estate cycle. Are values flat? Are values increasing? Are values decreasing? If they are decreasing, how far have they dropped at the point of your purchase? Does it appear they will drop further before they have bottomed out? It is a safe bet that if you plan on buying property and holding for the long-term, you will make money. However, speculating on a property's growth in value over the short-term is a gamble at best, and I would advise against it for the beginning investor.

This buildup of equity is closely associated with the term "appreciation." Appreciation is the act of an asset's value increasing. At the point of purchase, the property is acquired for Amount A. Over the years and over time, the value will potentially increase to Amount B (known as appreciation). Equity buildup is the positive difference or dollar amount between the two amounts. Note, equity buildup is described as such only when the value increases. When an asset's value decreases, there are all sorts of cool expressions to refer to an investor's unfortunate circumstances. "Taking a haircut" happens to be my favorite. All jokes aside, when things work out as planned and you have this increase in equity, you are on the path of progress to making additional investments and building your portfolio.

Like this…

Equity can be pulled from the property by way of a re-finance, more complexly referred to as repositioning the debt on the property. This refers to the debt position (payback period, interest rate and terms). Now, in the ideal situation, the equity buildup is used to purchase additional properties; however, it can also be used to enhance or improve the subject property. Additionally, equity buildup can be realized by sale of the subject property and subtracting the loan balance and any fees/commissions associated with the sale from the proceeds. The dollar amount leftover after the sale, loan payoff and payment of any sale-related expenses is your equity buildup.

Tax Shelter

Investing in real estate so that you can make money and shield other income from taxes? What a concept! And the IRS knows this is going on? YES! This is one of the oldest benefits in the book. Believe it or not, this was one of the primary reasons that investors acquired commercial real estate during the 1980s. Now, so far we have had a lagoon and a New York deli for our visual settings, so let's changes gears to…a jungle? Sure. Let's go.

There you are in the middle of a jungle. It's pouring down rain and you are dodging bullets, hand grenades and arrows as you see what appears to be a safe haven. You grab hold of a tree branch, leap to a vine, swing through the air and land on the front porch of a steel fort. It seems out of place, but you do not think twice as you swing the door open and walk in. Bullets, arrows and grenades ricochet off of the structure. Locking yourself inside the fort, you realize that this is just the shelter you needed. You are safe for the time being.

In our economy, with its progressive (or regressive, depending on how you see it) tax system, the hand grenades, arrows and bullets that were just being launched at you represent the taxes and regulations penalizing the wealthy, also read resourceful. But this steel fort represents the tax shelter provided to us by commercial real estate. Utilize the fort.

As the owner of commercial property, your tax benefits are plentiful. Referred to as a tax shelter, these benefits include: sheltering the income generated by the property, writing off the interest paid on the mortgage and deducting the depreciation, also known as cost recovery. These three benefits are separate in definition, but interlinked through their location in the financial equations associated with the tax benefits of owning commercial real estate.

Cost recovery, also known as depreciation, is perhaps the most appealing tax benefit to the commercial property owner as it does not incur an expense and therefore does not affect the property owner's cash flow. Depreciation is the act of deducting for the presumed decrease in your property's value. This benefit can in some scenarios shield the entirety of income generated at the property from taxes.

Mortgage interest is a large expense that is also tax deductible. In reviewing the following line-item breakdown of the aforementioned tax benefits, you will come to a better understanding of how closely related they are.

Example:

Gross Operating Income – Operating Expenses = Net Operating Income (Taxable)

Through the deductions allowed by the IRS, we can further reduce the taxable income through the following equation.

Net Operating Income – Mortgage Interest less Depreciation = New Taxable Income

When considered with real dollar amounts, these benefits are even more appealing to commercial property owners. Not only will you make money on your investment, you can shield a good portion of the income received from taxes.

Tax shelter is a benefit that you will receive any time you purchase commercial real estate. Note, as your net income decreases, so will your taxable income. If this taxable income becomes negative, you will have a loss to write-off. Should your net income decrease, through the reductions allowed by the IRS, you will have less taxable income than you would without the benefits of tax shelter. Use these benefits to your full advantage.

Hedge Against Inflation

Three down, one to go. Sticking with strange comparisons and/or picturesque settings, we will now take a cue from Kevin Costner. Who hasn't seen "Waterworld"? Ok, well maybe more of us can recall or quote "Field of Dreams", but nonetheless, follow me. Lakes, streams, oceans, rivers, aqueducts are flooding the world at a tremendous pace. Its Waterworld or close to it. Rather than risk being flooded and/or wiped out by the water, you decide to put up a dam to protect yourself. This is not any ordinary dam. This dam will actually grow higher as a result of the other dams growing around it, widening and rising higher. Building this dam not only saved you, but it allowed you to save your resources as well.

In this scenario, the dam you have constructed represents your investment in commercial real estate. The multiple bodies of water are the massive influx of printed money that inundates the economy during times of inflation. The other dams also growing are other commercial properties and assets that rise in value during times of inflation. So, as the water levels increase and rise higher, so does your dam, further shielding you from water damage. More money is available, so your real estate assets appreciate as a result.

Commercial real estate is perhaps the ideal hedge against inflation. As an asset, the value of real estate tends to rise along with other asset prices in the economy at large.

As such, in times of inflation there is too much money chasing after too few services; demand exceeds supply, and costs grow. Paper money depreciates or loses its value during inflationary times. Therefore, investing your money is not only smart, it is the safe thing to do. Additionally, the income brought in by commercial real estate is consistent and has the potential for growth over the long term. This potential growth in income serves as a cushion against a decline in real estate values. Real estate values may decrease in the short-term, but the rental income brought in remains steady.

Although the idea itself is complex, the benefits are quite easy to understand. Cash money loses its value as the value of assets increase. The value of your investment increases as the value of your cash decreases. What's more, investing in real estate provides you with periodic income to supplement your cash during inflationary times. As a hedge against inflation, commercial real estate is solid.

The Chain of Benefits
How do the investment goals function on their own vs. collectively?

Now that we know about the four benefits, we will understand the tandems, threesomes or foursomes that will essentially provide you with a more powerful, more potent real estate investment experience. You see, there is more to real estate than just cash flow, or appreciation. In the ideal situation, you can have your cake and eat it too. That is, you can strategically acquire real estate investments that will provide you with two, three or all four of the benefits and thus maximize your return on investment. But before you try to group or ungroup the benefits, it is important for you to understand why each of the aforementioned benefits or scenarios is important and how it will help you. Thus, understanding the aforementioned benefits of owning commercial real estate can help you determine the best investment scenario for you to pursue.

That said, it is important to realize that not all investment scenarios will satisfy the four benefits of owning commercial real estate. I can see how you might be confused, but you will soon understand. To use a non-real estate analogy, it's like going to the gym. You can go to lift weights and gain muscle, do cardio to burn calories or use your body weight to tone, or you could do a combination of cardio and weight lifting to burn fat. A physical trainer I am not, but now you understand the significance of these shared relationships.

How does this relate to real estate? Simple. You see, a property purchased for speculated appreciation and tax-shelter purposes might not yield positive cash flow short term and therefore would not satisfy the requirements of someone looking to supplement their wealth through passive income. And yet someone purchasing a property for cash flow purposes with the intent of holding the property over an extended period of time can expect to reap the benefits of appreciation, tax shelter and enjoy the hedge against inflation. We will now examine further the relationship between the four benefits.

The Cash flow Link

How will my investment for cash flow purposes allow me to enjoy the additional benefits of owning commercial real estate?

Purchasing a property for cash flow purposes is one of the safest and soundest acquisitions or investments that you can make. There are two main items to consider when buying for cash flow, including the purchase price and the income generated by the property. The income is ultimately what will cover the property's expenses, so it is important to evaluate the current, short-term and long-term income projections.

- What rents are in place now versus what is being achieved in the market area?
- How realistic are these rents in relation to the market area? Are they high/low?

Understanding the income will help you to underwrite an appropriate price at which to purchase or, more importantly, what you should walk away from purchasing.

To understand the amount of cash flow you will receive from your investment, you must consider: the purchase price, down payment, income received and terms of your financing. Remember, the net operating income (which is what is left in your net after shaking the operating expenses loose from the gross income) must pay for the debt service or financing. Whatever is left after you pay the debt service is your cash flow.

When buying for cash flow, the higher the income and the lower the debt service will bring you a greater cash flow. In buying for cash flow, you are guaranteed the benefits of tax shelter and a hedge against inflation. Should you hold the property for an extended period of time, it is likely that you receive the benefit of equity build-up or appreciation, although it is not guaranteed in the short-term.

Purchasing commercial real estate for cash-flow purposes with a long-term hold planned is the soundest real estate investment you can make.

The Equity Buildup/Appreciation Link

How will my investment for appreciation purposes allow me to experience additional benefits of owning commercial real estate?

Buying for appreciation is a safe bet over the long-term but is quite calculated and risky in the short term. Investors looking to realize equity buildup in the short-term must oftentimes are more hands-on and active in the management and maintenance of the property in order to achieve their goals. They will need to create intrinsic value that can be realized by the greater marketplace to then generate an inflated sales price once the property has been repositioned (redeveloped) and placed on the market.

The equity buildup investment scenario is guaranteed to provide the owner a hedge against inflation and tax shelter. Cash flow is possible depending on the income and terms of financing associated with the acquisition price, yet often the investor looking to buy for equity buildup is looking to:

1. purchase the property
2. introduce improvements
3. increase rents
4. sell the property and move on

As such, this scenario is speculative in nature and must be considered along with other aspects of the marketplace, including:

1. the availability of financing
2. the trending of rents
3. property values

A safe way to enjoy equity buildup/appreciation is to purchase for cash flow or tax-shelter purposes, thus planning for a long-term hold. This extended time period will allow more time for values to grow and as such, your equity will build as values climb over time as opposed to laboring to introduce value in the short-term.

Now that you are familiar with this aspect of the benefit, those late night infomercials will have less appeal. Remember, there is no short-cut to wealth. There are secrets, but not shortcuts.

The Tax Shelter Link
How will my investment for tax shelter purposes allow me to experience additional benefits of owning commercial real estate?

Tax shelter is a great addition or component to either the investment for cash flow or equity buildup purposes, but is not alone the sole best investment trigger for those with limited financial resources. Remember, tax shelter is the protection of your income through the sheltering of the taxes you pay. If you invest in real estate for the sole purpose of sheltering your taxes, you could potentially incur negative cash flow and be forced to come out of pocket to support or subsidize the property. So long as this is your intention, you are ok. Just be aware that this means you will be coming out of pocket to support the property rather than have the property support you. But when investing solely for tax shelter purposes, this is not an issue. You are looking to offset your income from other investments. Get it? A wiser bet is to look for positive cash flow real estate investments to receive the income AND the tax shelter. So before you decide on an investment strictly for tax-shelter purposes, you have some work to do. That is, you need to talk to your tax advisor.

Exploring these benefits with your CPA, you may learn that this may assist you in your current financial situation. However, for the beginning investor, tax shelter is best enjoyed as an added benefit of the investment for cash flow or long-term equity buildup scenarios.

The Hedge Against Inflation Link

How will my investment in real estate as a hedge against inflation allow me to experience the additional benefits of owning commercial real estate?

Investing in commercial real estate for the hedge against inflation it provides is quite similar to investing in real estate solely for tax shelter purposes. As such, the benefits of investing in real estate to enjoy the hedge against inflation that it provides are best when paired with the investment for cash flow, the investment for equity buildup or even when pairing it with the investment for tax shelter purposes.

This is another situation in which you should consult your CPA to understand how this investment will affect your overall financial well-being.

Determining What Type of Investor You Are
Questions to ask yourself and additional factors to consider

While many people acquire commercial real estate simply because they feel it will bring them more money or because it is a solid investment, it is important consider your goals, needs and wants. What are you attempting to achieve by investing your money in commercial real estate?

Take stock of your personal financial goals prior to investing. Essentially, picking the right investment scenario will assist you in getting to the next level of financial security. Therefore, it is imperative for you to understand where you are at in your life financially. What will better assist you in reaching financial success? We will now proceed through several groups of questions to help determine the appropriate investment for you to make.

Am I a cash-flow buyer?
What to ask and understand in determining whether or not you are investing for cash flow purposes.

Are you looking to supplement your monthly/quarterly income? If so, consider yourself a cash-flow buyer. Let me repeat myself again, but not for the last time. Buying for cash flow is the safest, soundest commercial real estate investment a person can make. What's more, the periodic disbursals of funds can assist with personal expenses or even be deposited into children's college funds for saving. It is your money;

you can do with it what you like. Boosting your spendable and savable income can be done through the strategic acquisition of commercial real estate for cash-flow purposes.

As a cash-flow buyer, you can expect to receive the added benefits of commercial real estate as a hedge against inflation, tax shelter benefits and depending on the hold term, equity buildup and appreciation. That's right: a smart cash-flow acquisition will yield you all four benefits of investing in commercial real estate.

Is the Investment For Equity Buildup Right For Me?
What to ask and understand in determining whether or not you should invest for equity buildup purposes

If you are looking to obtain in the future a lump sum of money upon the sale of a property perhaps after incurring out-of-pocket expenses to introduce improvements to it, you are buying for appreciation or equity buildup purposes. Note, in buying for appreciation, you will also receive the benefits of tax shelter and real estate as a hedge against inflation, but will not necessarily receive positive cash flow in the short-term. It is important to realize that while you will receive the tax shelter as you own the property, you will in fact have to pay taxes on any proceeds received from the sale of the property. For this reason, many real estate owners choose to facilitate what is known as a 1031 Tax Deferred Exchange. Do not confuse yourself in the short-term; that only applies to the proceeds from a sale. What a 1031 Exchange allows you to do is trade or your roll your basis and proceeds into the purchase of a property of equal to or greater value, and as a result, pay no taxes on the gains and keep the basis from your previous asset. This is a valuable tool and you should be sure to explore this option with your tax advisor upon the sale of your real estate holdings. We will explore this concept later in the book.

Investors interested in improving the property for sale in the near term are interested in appreciation and might not be interested in cash flow generated by the property over the holding period as their focus is on the proceeds to be generated by the sale of the property. Can I support the property? Can I fund improvements to introduce value to the property? After introducing these improvements, am I looking to sell for profit? If so, I am buying for equity buildup and appreciation.

Tax Benefits and a Hedge Against Inflation
What you need to know about these added benefits

Tax shelter and a hedge against inflation are provided by commercial real estate. In fact, when acquiring a property either for cash flow or for appreciation purposes, you will also receive the benefits of tax shelter and a hedge against inflation. Someone buying commercial real estate for its tax shelter and hedge against inflation benefits is similar to the person buying for appreciation purposes since the property does not necessarily generate income sufficient to cover the expenses incurred by the property, and as such, the investor must come out of pocket to cover the expenses.

Although this signifies negative cash flow, it is in fact a tax benefit as you are coming out of pocket to subsidize the property's expenses, thus spending down your personal income. If you are looking to protect a portion of your personal income from taxes, consider investing in commercial real estate. As for the inflation benefits, simply ask yourself, "Can I afford to lose money that I have worked hard for and saved due to the excess printing and availability of paper money in the marketplace?" If the answer is no, consider investing in commercial real estate, since it not only appreciates in times of inflation but ultimately increases your net worth as a result.

Where to Go and How to Proceed
Whom to know, whom to consult and what to consider with regard to your commercial real estate investment

As an investor, it is important to align yourself with like-minded professionals who share in your goals for success. A fruitful acquisition requires your interaction with a financial institution, a CPA privy to the ins and outs of the numerous tax benefits as they relate to commercial real estate, an attorney specializing in estate planning, a real estate broker and, depending on the size/location of the property, a professional property-management firm.

Talk to your CPA or accountant. Are they familiar with the many tax benefits and loopholes associated with commercial property? If not, can they refer you to an accountant or CPA who is? The same goes for your attorney. If you have a family attorney, discuss with them your potential acquisition and ask for them to recommend to you an attorney who will help organize the appropriate will/trust to prevent headaches down the line.

In looking for financing, first approach your financial institution or bank. Does it provide financing for commercial real estate acquisitions? If not, does it have a branch that does? In some cases, dealing with a financial institution with which you already have a relationship will yield better results, optimal rates and/or save you fees. If not, study some of the recently closed transactions in your market area to find out who provided the most attractive financing on transactions most similar to yours. Proceed in interviewing the financier and determine the best fit for your goals.

Do your homework and ensure yourself that these professionals truly represent your best interests and are not simply looking to make a quick buck and move on. It is important to realize that a real estate broker works on a commission-only pay-scale. As such, they do not make money unless something is sold. Scrutinize any financial data, spreadsheets or documentation furnished to you by a real estate broker, since it may not always contain the most accurate, relevant or current financial data. If you do not yet know what to scrutinize, you will learn during the "DDDR" portion of this book.

Survey the area around the property you are looking to purchase and write down the company names that you see on signs of properties that appear to be professionally managed. Do you observe signs of deferred maintenance? Are vacancies well advertised? Are the grounds neatly kept? Does the property exude pride of ownership? Obtain a list of three to five companies and arrange to meet with them to interview and evaluate their credentials. Are they licensed/bonded/insured? Are they members of the Institute of Real Estate Management? In retaining professional management services, you are entrusting your investment to someone whose performance and ability to maximize income and curb expenditures has a direct impact on your bottom line.

One thing to keep in mind is that you do not have to go it alone. Group investments are great for the beginning investor. Often sponsored or syndicated by real estate investment firms, these group investments offer the investor the unique ability to own a portion of a large piece of property with greater income potential while not involving or requiring of them the hands-on management that is associated with becoming the sole owner of a commercial property. Again, it is important to evaluate the firm's track record, credentials and qualifications in addition to understanding whether or not the firm's goals are in sync or simpatico with your own.

Investing in commercial real estate can be the foundation for your financial security or a building block in your quest for wealth. Whatever role it plays, it is important to consider your goals and understand how you intend to make your real estate investment the vehicle toward

making them a reality. Now that you know the four benefits of investing in commercial real estate, you are capable of determining the best
investment scenario and can effectively proceed in selecting an investment that will meet your criteria and help you reach your goals. During
the next portion of this book, we will discuss the acquisition or investment process, and you will learn how to acquire the type of investment
opportunity in which you are interested.

INVESTOR PROFILE

Name: Jim

Prior Occupation: Miscellaneous Hourly Jobs

Started Investing at Age: 18

First Investment: Two side-by-side fourplexes with $10k down

Current Real Estate Holdings: Over 100 Units across multiple properties

Why Real Estate: More control over my investments. Leverage, creative financing, the ability to create or add value as well as the tax benefits are all reasons I like real estate.

I Wish I Knew When I Started That: Tenant screening is important and failing to do so can lead to evictions, property damage, rent losses and other unfortunate occurrences. My dad was my mentor, which was mostly good, but I unfortunately picked up some of his bad habits. This was one of them.

What I Look For in an Investment: I like to own properties near where I live so that I can keep an eye on them. I either buy stabilized properties in good areas and hold for the long-term or purchase property with value-add potential for short or long-term holds.

To Those Starting Out, I Say: Find a strong mentor or join a local real estate group. Read books, such as the "Rich Dad" series and attend conferences or seminars. Browse Realtor.com, Loopnet and start early! Don't analyze forever, take a calculated risk and jump in. Buy a duplex or fourplex and run it yourself for at least two years to learn the business from the ground up.

NICHOLAS A. DUNLAP

CHAPTER 3:
It's All About the Numbers

"You've got be very careful if you don't know where you're going, because you might not get there!"

YOGI BERRA

In Hollywood, it's all about who you know. Actors and their agents run in relatively small social and professional circles, and as a result, the more well-connected stars get the most work or even the best work. Real estate is not much different, but in real estate, it's sort of a combination of what you know and how long it takes for you to act on what you know. Thus, knowledge and timing are everything. Knowing how to identify a prime investment opportunity and knowing how to move on it quickly can be the difference between having a one-asset portfolio and a 20-asset portfolio.

While every investor has his or her own set of requirements for the performance of their real estate holdings—or more specifically, their expectation for the returns on their real estate investments—it is important to remember a few things as we begin to tackle this most important aspect of the business. First, understand that there is tons of money in this world, more than you can imagine. So much money that, in fact, if you or I actually knew how much was out there, we would be amazed. So, realize that people who will be competing with you for these investment opportunities will potentially have more money at their disposal than you do. If so, they can or will likely tolerate lower returns. And you know what? Let them have their lower returns. There are plenty of opportunities out there for us all to build and develop our wealth.

Building your portfolio from one asset to 20 assets is not difficult. Generally speaking, the most difficult acquisition to make will be your first. But in going from one to 20, you will improve your skills and fix the kinks in your real estate investment and management operation along the way.

Now that you know the reasons behind investing and you are acquainted with the four benefits, let's discover the two sets of numbers that will become equally as important to you as, let's say, your social security number, your spouse's cell phone number and your birthdate. And actually, these numbers might even be more important because you really only have one shot at getting them right. That is, if you mess up your numbers "going in" or on the acquisition, you are going to have a harder time getting the asset to perform once you own it.

When buying residential real estate, it is all about the emotion connected with living in that space: the feeling you have when you wake up, make breakfast, tuck your children in and shut the light off at night. With investment real estate, you cannot let emotion rule. Repeat to yourself over and over, "I am a smart investor, and I make intelligent decisions with my finances. My emotions do not affect my investment decisions."

Good. Now say it one more time: "I am a smart investor, and I make intelligent decisions with my finances. My emotions do not affect my investment decisions."

With that, you will now learn of or come to understand two sets of numbers. One set is based on the financial return that you will receive on a given investment, and the other is based on the market value of an investment. Although the two sets of numbers represent different aspects of your underwriting and can stand alone, they are also inter-linked. We will review their relationship below.

Cost measures and **investment measures**: two different sets of numbers for two different parts of the underwriting and financial analysis part of the acquisition. Understanding why these numbers are important and how they are linked together will make you an extremely successful investor. Failing to understand their relationship can cost you a lot of money, your credit score and possibly even some serious time in the doghouse from your significant other for making a poor financial decision and jeopardizing your livelihood. We want to avoid such blunders. So, how do you measure up?

Cost Measures

A cost measure is specifically based on the market price or sales price and is relative to every single asset-specific measurement possible. For apartments, that would mean: cost per unit, cost per room and one of the most important measures: cost per square foot. Cost per square foot is unique and that you can compare between asset classes, be it multifamily, retail, office or industrial. The cost per square foot will allow you to quickly determine where if all things are equal, you might get the best value on your investment. For office buildings, this would be more along the lines of cost per square foot, cost per rentable square foot and cost per floor.

To arrive at these highly useful cost measures, you simply divide the purchase price by the total number of the statistic or measure that you are trying to find. It is quite simple.

Cost Per Unit = Purchase Price/Total Units

Cost Per Room = Purchase Price/Total Bedrooms

Cost Per Square Foot = Purchase Price/Total square feet

Cost Per Rentable Square Feet = Purchase Price/ Rentable Square feet

Cost Per Floor = Purchase Price/Number of Floors

Knowing these numbers and how to arrive at and interpret them quickly as they relate to the investment you are considering will allow you to determine a number of things, including: whether the owner is smoking some good stuff and the property will never sell at that price, whether the property is priced within your striking range or even that the property is priced so low that you need to move now. It's all in the numbers.

Investment Measures

Just like cost measures are based on how much something costs on its per-measurement basis, investment measures provide the same sort of detail. Investments, however, are based on the correlative financial return on the subject property at a specific price.

It is important to realize that just like there are different cost measures to be aware of, there are different investment measures of which to be aware and with which to be familiar. As you understand what you are looking to accomplish with your real estate investment goals, you will be better equipped to move on the opportunities available in the marketplace.

So, just what are these investment measures?

Capitalization Rate (Cap Rate)

Better known as the "Cap Rate" or "Cap," the capitalization rate uses the Net Operating Income produced by an asset and compares it to the market value of the specific asset. So, to arrive at the capitalization rate you simply divide the Net Operating Income by the purchase price. Yes, you are looking for a percentage. Simply put, the Cap Rate is the yield on a particular investment if you were to pay all cash.

One good thing to keep in mind is that when you are investing, it is a best practice to use leverage to your advantage. Leverage, of course, means that you are using someone else's money to your benefit; in most cases, this will be a bank's money. At a glance, when your capitalization rate is higher than the interest rate on the loan that you have received to purchase the asset, you are in a positive leverage situation. And thus, borrowing money will actually enhance the financial return you receive on your investment. Remember when I talked about my dad's talk with me as a kid on the way to school? OPM? Well, this is OPM. And with the right investment, this leverage will kick your financial return or yield into overdrive.

Cap rates are subjective as they are based on the operating expenses incurred by the property or more specifically by the operator of the property. For this reason, I prefer to make my own blend of the NOI by reviewing and adjusting the numbers presented by a broker or an owner. There will be ways I can improve upon what they do and there will also be expenses that they do not factor into the equation.

Don't ever take the numbers at face value. They have been massaged to look good. That is, there will expenses that have been excluded, minimized or skimped on here. Don't worry; we will discuss this at length in the Winning Property Management Strategies portion of the book (Part III).

Gross Rent Multiplier (GRM)

So if the Cap Rate is a subjective number that has likely been mas-saged by a slick broker looking for a quick deal, the Gross Rent Multi-plier or GRM is just the opposite. The GRM tells you, in short, how many years it will take the current gross rents to pay back the purchase price; thus, the lower the number the better.

A GRM of 13 means that in 13 years, the property will "gross" enough rent to pay off the purchase price. Of course, these are gross figures and do not account for the expenses that will need to be paid, but that's fine! Gross figures allow an experienced operator to understand and quickly identify upside potential in rents and also speculate on or put together pro-forma expense figures. The Cap Rate would require some work to pick apart the NOI and then unbundle or reconfigure the expenses. With the GRM and the gross figures, you have all the data you need.

There is also a spin-off of this figure, and that is the GIM or Gross Income Multiplier. The GIM accurately takes into account the receipt of any ancillary sources of income: utility reimbursements, promotional partnerships, laundry income, parking income, etc. If anything, the GIM is the more beneficial number to use; just be sure to differentiate between the two figures so that you do not confuse yourself or your investors. You will soon have enough investment acronyms in your vocabulary to make a bowl of alphabet soup.

Cash on Cash ($/$ %) / Return on Investment (ROI)

If real estate investment measures had a cleanup hitter, a knockout artist, a black belt or a gold medalist in the category, it would most cer-tainly be the **cash-on-cash** rate of return. Simple to figure and simple to understand, the Cash-on-Cash rate of return or $/$ is quite simply the percentage rate of cash being returned on the total cash invested.

To arrive at the $/$, we annualize the before-tax cash flow and divide it by the total amount you have invested into the asset.

$/$ % = Before-Tax Cash Flow (annualized amount)/ Total Investment

As you can see, this is your total investment—not the total purchase price. This is an equity measure of sorts and it can help to determine whether your **return on investment** in a specific real estate transaction will provide you a superior or inferior return in comparison to other asset classes such as: stocks, bonds or commodities. For this reason, ROI is like the granddaddy of real estate investing measures.

Each investment measure is both relevant and or significant in its own way, but if I had to rank them in order of importance to you in your search, I would rank them as follows:

1. cash on cash
2. gross rent multiplier
3. capitalization rate

Of course, there are far more complex, sophisticated measures of return, but why drive yourself crazy? If you know the aforementioned three returns, you will know more than enough to aid in making your decision of whether or not to proceed with a potential acquisition.

As you seek out investment opportunities, you will want to run either Microsoft Excel or Apple Numbers. These software programs will allow you to create highly formulized spreadsheets that will assist in arriving at both the investment and cost measures with ease. And like Peter Drucker once said, "What gets measured gets done." This is entirely true in real estate investment.

Talk about a numbers game. Real estate investment is all about the numbers: knowing when to move on a particular property and when to pass on a property. The only way to truly know these numbers is to constantly seek out, identify opportunities and underwrite them. Underwrite until you hate spreadsheets so much that you never want to see one again. And then, go write another spreadsheet or two. Really, people! It's all about the numbers!

You may ask, "You mean it's not all about location?" Of course not! Not all of it. Sure, a large portion of the value of real estate of any kind is location, but income property is income property. You are buying a business. You are buying an income stream. It is important to understand the quality of the income stream associated with the asset. Look for good, constant quality, and look for high quality. Oftentimes, there will be a correlation between a strong location and higher income stream, but realize that you will pay a premium for that location and will not always achieve a correlative financial return.

Putting It All Together

So now that we know what to look for and we can determine what is a good buy or bad buy and understand how to compare our figures to those of recently sold, currently available or pending in-escrow transactions, let's talk about something that will make your life a heck of a lot easier. This magical tool I speak of is known as the **spreadsheet**.

Just like no two investors are equal, no two acquisition spreadsheets are equal. With that, there are fundamental measures and figures that should be included on each spreadsheet. A spreadsheet should be as simple or as sophisticated as the investor. If you are simply looking to achieve a certain cash-on-cash rate of return, then you do not need sexy measures of future equity growth. So, what basics should you include? These figures are included below:

Figures to Include on Your Spreadsheet

- current rents
- potential rents
- purchase price
- down payment
- loan amount and terms (life/interest rate/points/etc)
- operating expenses
- cost measures
- investment measures

If you start with these fundamentals, you can add on as much detail or data as you'd like, simplify the layout as much as you like and dress it up or down as you please. It is important to remember that you will want to be able to key in the asset-specific numbers easily and have the pre-formulized cells auto-update with the new dollar amounts. Depending on how much work you do ahead of time, this can really save time when it counts.

For a real estate investor, a good spreadsheet is almost like a mechanic looking under the hood or a doctor checking one's vital signs. You will be able to identify problems quickly, tighten up loose screws, check the oil and understand whether to proceed or do a little more work first. In the appendix section of this book, you will find a sample acquisition form that I have prepared. It is basic, it is simple and it does the trick. (Sometimes, less is more. Don't confuse yourself with extraneous detail when trying to focus on isolated, specific numbers.)

Throughout the course of this book, you will notice that certain phrases or ideas get repeated. And that is because these phrases are *uber* important. In real estate, you make your money when you buy. Knowing the numbers will allow you to negotiate the best purchase price and "going in" strategy possible. This will only help you as your pro-forma numbers start to become a reality. And if these pro-forma numbers do not become a reality, it will not matter, because you have not over-speculated. Instead, you have cautiously underwritten, consulted your spreadsheet and familiarized yourself with both the cost and investment measures. One of the biggest differences between purchasing residential and commercial real estate is the level of emotion that is involved in the acquisition process.

Buying a home is all about the emotional value. Investing in an income property is all about the financial return coming back to the investor. Just like your emotional needs and wants will drive the purchase of a residential property, financial gain will drive your investment in commercial real estate. Remember to pay attention to the interlinked relationship between the cost measures as they relate to your investment measures. Understand how they play off of one another and do not allow your emotions to cloud your spreadsheet.

Numbers don't lie. Remember that!

· · · · · · · · · · · · · · · · · · ·

PART II:

Due Diligence and Underwriting Done Right

· · · · · · · · · · · · · · · · · · ·

NICHOLAS A. DUNLAP

CHAPTER 4:

Becoming the Marketplace Mastermind

"Knowledge speaks, but wisdom listens."

JIMI HENDRIX

As you read in Chapter 1, you make your money in commercial real estate going in, or in other words, on the acquisition. Since the numbers are paramount when it comes to investing, knowing the marketplace is key to your success.

Now, knowing your marketplace breaks down once again to two sets of numbers. Those numbers are the **rental comps** (short for rental comparable data) and the **sales comps** (sales comparable data). Both are interlinked and share a unique relationship. What makes this relationship unique is that commercial real estate is valued on the quality and quantity of income that it produces. The income produced or generated is the rent and other income, and the market value is the sales data. Essentially, higher rents equal higher market values and sales prices.

Here, you will want to understand the who, what, where, when and why behind the investment and also behind the occupancy. This will help you not only to be more aware while you are in acquisition mode, but also later when you are in operator mode. Knowing who rents what space and how much of that space they rent for what cost and for how long matters. Facts are important, and they are easy to find out. All it takes is the right relationships and the right tools. Real estate is almost like a craft in that it requires an investor to compile a tool box with all the right tools and supplies. None of these tools is simpler than market knowledge. But it takes time, dedication and the ability to build relationships.

Are you up for it? Of course you are. But before you get into the data collection, research and analysis portion of your due diligence, it is important to understand the different types of income properties and their corresponding markets. The system is quite simple and uses nothing more than a letter-grade system, similar to schools.

The Letter Grade

First things first. Each market is different in that there are C- through AAA rankings. However, one market's B property could be another market's A property and could also be another market's C property. That is, the scale is entirely subjective based on interior and exterior amenities as well as the immediate location within the sub-market and market.

So, start wide and tailor it down. Grade the market as a whole, grade the sub-market surrounding your property and then grade your property. In Los Angeles, a vintage garden-style community built in the 1960s will likely be a C+ class property, whereas a AAA is going to mean virtually brand-new construction with a number of luxurious amenities. Now, obviously there are a number of different neighborhoods in the city that will have a significant impact on the price as well. A C+ building in a C area is worth less than a C+ building in an A area.

See what I mean? The system itself is simple. The more complex task is becoming comfortable with the individual neighborhoods and areas, understanding the nuances of the rental submarket within which the property is located. Once you have a solid grasp on the neighborhood and area, you will be able to differentiate between building and area class with ease. This will help you to accurately and efficiently digest the rental and sales data that you receive.

If you are looking at C-class buildings, it is important to understand C-class values and C-class rents. It is also important to understand where B and A class rents and values are as well. This will help you to ensure that you do not overpay for the particular asset that you are considering. If after thorough research and detailed review of the market and sub-market within question, reach out to your broker or lender and ask for the classification of the neighborhood. Although the data will be subjective, it is important to rely on and learn from professionals as you learn for yourself.

Sales Data

Now, a commercial real estate broker can be your best friend or your worst nightmare, a valuable member of your investment team or your own personal Max Cady of Cape Fear fame. Since we would all prefer the first of these two options in both scenarios, it is important to choose accordingly. The signs are out there. You just have to look closely.

The Internet makes things increasingly convenient for investors. In additional to traditional Multiple Listing Services available mostly to real estate professionals, today, investors have access to a website known as Loopnet (http://www.loopnet.com). Loopnet allows investors to research agents, available commercial properties as well as current and recent market activity. As you browse Loopnet and search for properties within the geographic region and property type that you are looking for, note the brokers that you see again and again. You will likely notice that one or two, maybe three brokers depending on the size of the market will dominate the listings and available inventory. These are the brokers which whom you will want to make contact. Reach out to them via telephone or email and ask to take them to coffee to discuss the market.

Now, I may be old fashioned, but I still prefer a quick and in-person meeting. At this meeting, you will want to introduce yourself and explain to the broker what you are looking for: property type/size/location/financial return/etc. Plus, commercial real estate is a business that is known as a shark pool. A face-to-face meeting can help to determine whether or not the person you are going to be doing business with is trustworthy or not. Once you have provided the broker with this information, you will want to make sure that they either show you their own listings or off-market inventory. Commercial real estate is not like residential real estate in that there will not always be a commission paid to a cooperating broker. So guess who can get stuck with the bill? YOU.

So don't stress, don't worry, don't panic; just be careful! Be aware.

Just like the broker will bring you investment opportunities that fit your interest, they should also be a resource when it comes to finding out what things sold for, what things are selling for, what is available and what is coming online in the near future. Brokers thrive on relationships and can provide you with a wealth of information.

Loopnet allows investors to access information not only on what is available for purchase, but also on comparable sales and lease data, which includes the availability of space for lease. This is a big resource for investors, so be sure to use it to your advantage. In fact, if you were to consider Loopnet a tool within your toolbox, consider it a Swiss Army knife with a variety of uses. Know how to use it to your advantage.

Now, although I am old-school in my approach to relationship building, I realize the importance of leveraging technology in my approach to investing. You should too.

What's on the Market?

With our real estate broker working full-time on finding potential acquisitions, we are able to continue our own search while pursuing additional market knowledge, expertise and available investment opportunities. You will come to realize that there is insight and information that will help you almost as much as your financial resources will when it comes to investing. You are reading this book, so you obviously have the financial resources and the corresponding intelligence level. Now, let's discuss some of the additional ways to find the opportunities available in the marketplace.

While most of today's brokers will advertise their commercial real estate listings on Loopnet, some are pre-advertised in the business classified or real estate section of your local newspaper. This can be a great way to find out about an opportunity before the property is actually placed on one of the major outlets such as Loopnet or the MLS. These classified ads do not run every day, so it is important to find out when the real estate listings in your area will publish. Depending on the opportunity, you may need to act fast. Be sure to know your data. You'll want to have your spreadsheet ready.

Aside from the classifieds, you will want to communicate with your broker network to find out about their new listings, listings that they are working on or the off-market or "know-about" listings of which they may be aware. In these instances, a broker will appreciate your ability to move quickly and keep things confidential as they will not want to jeopardize a potential listing should the transaction fall apart.

The ability to provide this comfort will often allow you a first look at some of the freshest, most lucrative opportunities.

Be sure to put in the time and build the relationship. It will pay off!

Again, Loopnet is a great source for any and all available for-sale commercial real estate. The site is easily accessible and offers both a free membership with limited access and a subscription membership with a nominal fee. The latter offers access to all of the listings and resources that Loopnet has to offer. While in acquisition mode, it will be of great use for you to purchase the premium membership.

Both through brokers and through your review of comparable sales data, you will be able to form an understanding of what properties are selling for in your desired area, and better yet, you will be able to identify what stands out as or what you perceive to be a "good buy." With these prices and addresses in mind, you will be able to prepare a spreadsheet with the data so that you can quickly and conveniently compare the properties that you are so feverishly underwriting to those properties that have recently sold.

It is important to understand how the properties compare. Are the physical location, amenities and financial return similar? If so, where is your property in terms of a superior or inferior position? Be honest with yourself and be accurate. Of course, if you have questions, you can always discuss your opinion with a broker or even a lender. While we will discuss the important role that a lender will play in the acquisition process later on in the book, it is important to understand here that a lender will tell you whether your price is on the mark or short of it, whether obtaining financing will be of ease or will require additional work.

Yes, real estate is not just about numbers and location; it is also about relationships. If you can focus on those three things, you will become quite successful in your ventures. Another thing to remember is that realistic expectations go a long way when it comes to investing. So, if you are having a hard time locating your desired return, your desired price or your desired terms, go back and have another look at the comparable sales data to see how much similar properties in the area are really fetching and make sure that you have realistic expectations.

Rental Rates

Just as you surveyed the for-sale and recently sold data to assist in your understanding of the market, your survey of the rental rates on properties comparable to your own will be of equal importance. Knowing where rents are at on the property of interest versus the properties in the competitive marketplace allows you to understand the upside potential (if any) in the existing rents. The rental survey is a tool that you should also insert into your acquisition toolbox.

Here again, you will want to consult multiple sources for the data you are seeking. Start with your broker, but be sure to verify independently the data with which you are presented.

Next, for office/commercial real estate, you can consult websites such as Loopnet.com and CoStar. Then, do your own search online by checking sites such as Craigslist, For Rent and Apartment Guide. Lastly, drive the immediate neighborhood, outlying neighborhood and greater area around the property. Write down any telephone numbers, addresses and building names and follow up with a telephone call.

The rental survey is a very simple process. Essentially, you are comparing the units or space at the subject property to its competitors. Thus, you will need to spend time collecting the imperative data on the competing properties. This data includes but is not limited to:

- unit type (bed/bath) – square footage
- interior upgrades – amenities
- utilities paid (yes/no) – exterior/common areas

Most importantly, you want to know the rents and security deposits being charged on rented space. You will likely be surprised in that you will meet other owners and or managers in the process and as a result, you will gain a unique insight into the rental activity within a neighborhood or sub-market of which you would not have otherwise been aware. Being cognizant of these trends as you approach your investment will help you understand what you need to do keep up with, get ahead of or be slightly more profitable than your competitors.

Keep your rental comparable data handy. You will utilize this information again and again throughout the course of your ownership. We will further discuss the significance of complete, concise and timely rental surveys during the WPMS portion of the book.

Now that you know the details on the sold and for-sale market, as well as the leased and for lease market, you will become more in tune with the synergistic relationship between the for lease and for sale numbers. The rental survey will help you understand how to price your product in order to minimize vacancy, maximize your income, beat the market, meet the market or just keep up with the market. The more information you have available, the better.

Strength in Numbers

Mario and Luigi. Simon and Garfunkle. Cheech and Chong. Calvin and Hobbes. Magic and Kareem. Batman and Robin. OK, you get it: duos, synergy. The relationship between rental data and sales data is equally important because due to the fact that you can either afford to pay more or less for a property based on the income being brought in or the income that could potentially be brought in. And just as the for-sale market has cycles, so does the rental market.

At times when the rental market is depressed, the for-sale market will also be down. It is important to look for identify that correlation. You don't want to overpay for the income that you will be receiving. If rental rates have been trending upward, you can expect to make more. Look for that same correlation if and when rental rates on a certain property type happen to be on a downward-sliding scale. Make sure that you have a good, solid grasp on the trailing 12 to 24 months of operation within the market and whether or not rental rates have increased, declined or held steady. This will help you to understand how whether you should continue to consider the investment and if you should decide to, how aggressive your investment or acquisition strategy will be.

As you become comfortable with the different markets and sub-markets and understand the values of different classes of buildings in different areas, you will realize that your investment barometer or gauge is much sharper. You will be able to identify the investment opportunities that are of interest quickly and effectively. Remember, timing is very important in this business. Prime investment opportunities often require an investor to move swiftly. Being the market expert will help you to move on these opportunities.

INVESTOR PROFILE

Name: Mary

Prior Occupation: Homemaker

Started Investing at Age: 40

First Investment: It was sort of a chain of events, but we purchased a triplex and then traded into 10 units; then, we sold our house and traded the 10 units into a 22 unit building which we later refinanced and then bought a 30 unit building. From 3 units, we ended up with 52 units total.

Current Real Estate Holdings: 15 Units and a 3 rental houses

Why Real Estate: It is a tangible asset with controllability not offered by other asset classes. In the physical sense, you have something to touch and something to work with. With stocks and with other markets, it's all imaginary. You have no control over any of the operations.

I Wish I Knew When I Started That: Stick to what you know. Having participated in a number of transactions, we felt somewhat savvy or sophisticated and decided to participate in ground-up development. Fortunately, we made it out OK, but we should have just stuck with the acquisition and disposition of existing multifamily product.

What I Look For in an Investment: When I was younger, I looked for equity growth or buildup potential, which is somewhat speculative. Now, as a retiree, I am interested more in cash flow and stability.

To Those Starting Out, I Say: Just start! Somehow, some way, whether it's a duplex, partnership or rental house…Just start! Eliminate the obstacles you might be facing and go for it! Starting small can help, so explore your options and start NOW! Be willing to take calculated risks, but do not buy in the red.

CHAPTER 5:
Let's Get Physical

"It's the little details that are vital. Small things make a big difference."

JOHN WOODEN

The physical component to due diligence is equally important although slightly less subjective and more about the facts—as in: your assessment of the area, your assessment of the property and any deferred maintenance, roof issues, plumbing issues, landscape condition, necessary improvements, etc. Just like you will consult with professionals during your financial-analysis portion of due diligence, you will also consult with professionals here. Only here, the professionals are contractors, plumbers, repairmen and the like. Yes, this acquisition vendor list will be added to your acquisition toolbox.

Going in to your acquisition, you want to be fully aware and have full understanding of any deficiencies in the building's operating systems (plumbing, electrical, gas, HVAC) and you want to know whether you should ask the seller for some of these costs before you make the purchase, whether you will have to adjust your offer price and whether the issues are so severe that you should in fact step back from or consider cancelling the transaction. While I cannot decide for you as to whether or not you should cancel the purchase, I can certainly provide you with advice.

First Things First

Prior to ever making an offer and beginning your financial due diligence, you want to drive the neighborhood and at the very least walk around the perimeter of the property. At this point in time, you are getting a feel for the property, whether you feel safe in the neighborhood and whether or not this is the type of place that you will not mind coming to after hours, on weekends or in a rush to make a quick or inexpensive repair or meet a tenant. Of course, it will also help you arrive at an understanding of where to start your negotiations on the potential purchase.

It is important not to disturb the tenants and not to let them know that you are considering purchasing the property or more importantly that the property is on the market. If you happen to get spotted or someone asks you what you are doing, just play dumb. Keep quiet. Eventually, the resident or manager will leave you alone. Exterior inspection only at this point in time and it is really intended just to give you a feel for the property.

On this initial inspection or site visit, you are looking at things like wood, stucco, windows, paint, landscape, garages, gates, concrete, paving and making notes of anything that you might have questions on or that you might think could cost money to fix. This is not your walk-through and this is not your physical inspection; this is simply your first site visit. That said, it is important to make it count. So take good notes and highlight any big concerns that you have. Should you proceed with making an offer, you will want to call in a professional that specializes in that work.

Now, if you notice that there is wood and stucco repair and that the building could use a touch-up or new paint, then consider that prior to making your offer. Price out what that work should cost and factor it in to your purchase price. From a strategy perspective, you are better to take it off of your purchase price than leave it in and ask for it back. Leaving it in and then asking for it back has the psychological effect of a seller conceding, losing money or giving back money. And nobody likes to lose money.

Interior Inspections

Having now conducted your initial site visit and tour prior to making an offer or quite possibly even before reaching out to the listing broker, it is now time for you to take the next step. And that is either making an offer to gain entrance into a select number of interiors (on a larger building) or on a smaller building, seeing inside of each apartment home or office suite. At this point in time, it is strongly suggested that you have a general contractor attend the walk-through with you. A general contractor should have a very strong working knowledge of all aspects of the local building code and as a result, they are qualified to assist with questions regarding electrical, plumbing, structural concerns, you name it. Although this contractor may not be the contractor that you hire to ultimately do the work, you can rely on their skill and expertise during the due diligence process.

As you enter into each apartment home, be sure to take detailed notes of any repairs you feel are necessary, make notes of any upgrades that you feel might be necessary and then, snap a picture with your cell phone and make a note to reference the photo. This will help to jog your memory when you have completed the inspection and are in need of a reference point. While your general contractor will be focusing more on the significant red flags, you will want to focus on the seemingly simple yet ever so helpful aspects of the walk-through.

Look under the sinks in the kitchens and bathrooms, look for any plumbing problems, look for mold issues, look for signs of pest control issues. And while each unit will in fact be different, it is a best practice to draw up a walk-through spreadsheet ahead of time that accurately accounts for the following information:

- unit number – unit type – plumbing checked (any issues?)
- pest issues (list) – mold issues (list) – overall condition of unit

Another thing to consider is that while you can ask a dirty tenant to clean up, a filthy tenant who has food particles and other perishable items scattered across the apartment in a seemingly hoarder-like fashion, well, you will likely want to ask them to leave once you own the building. So take a note of that as well!

Speaking of residents, take the time to endear yourself to the residents politely and professionally as you enter into their apartment. Ask them if you can look around. Ask if there is anyone else home. Compliment them on their design, their style, their furniture, their pasta that they are cooking for lunch. You get the picture. Come across as a nice person, not the greedy bastard looking to crank their rent as soon as you close escrow. Even if that is exactly what you want to do, you do not have to be a jerk about it. Always say goodbye and thank residents for allowing you to enter inside of their space. True, if they are provided with notice they do not have a choice, but being polite never hurt anyone, right?

Do you get it? You are applying your common sense to the inspection and understanding what is physical and what is operational. What is expensive and what is inexpensive. You are also making notes of what you will want to have an expert come back through and look at going forward. Even if it is unlikely the seller will issue a credit or adjust the purchase price in your favor, it is wise for you to have an expert address the issues.

Of course, while the general contractor is on the property you will want to make sure that they assess the exterior as well. Look inside any of the garages, look at the eaves, the fascia, the roof, the stucco, the wood, the metal, the decks, the stairs—you name it. You need to walk away from the initial walk-through with a true understanding of whether or not you will be proceeding with the investment. Having a reliable and trustworthy general contractor with you will help you to not under or over-estimate what a specific repair might cost. Often times, a real estate investment neophyte will enter into an apartment or office acquisition as though they are purchasing a home. Not only will this help to prevent their purchase of income property, they will alienate their network of brokers and other professionals who will soon realize…

> "This person doesn't know what they're doing! I am not
> bringing them a deal ever again!"
> — bothered broker

Reconciling After the Interior Inspection

OK, so now that you have you finished your inspection and you have detailed notes and photos on each of the items of concern, it is time to contact the specific vendors who will assist with necessary work. Call your plumber, electrician and handyman and explain to them the issues. You should be able to get a fairly accurate cost estimate over the phone simply by providing them with detail. However, you will want a precise estimate for any bargaining or negotiation, so it will be a good idea to schedule a second due diligence trip back to the property.

Realize that tenants must be provided with notice any time that you enter into the rented space. So be mindful of this as you attempt to schedule your trips. This will make things easier on the broker, management company and/or the owner. As part of the negotiation process, you will want to somewhat endear yourself to the owner. You do not want to be known as the jerk that made him write up a notice and distribute it to the tenants, only to have you ask to reschedule or not show up. Line up your vendors, and hit the property hard. These precise numbers are one of the final items that you will need to complete your pre-acquisition spreadsheet.

Although we will talk a lot about the importance of doing business with trustworthy vendors in the WPMS portion of the book, I really cannot stress how important it is to not only know who you are doing business with but to know that they will not take you for a ride. Accurate pricing is of the utmost importance because the difference between $5k and $10k can in some cases make all the difference.

CHAPTER 6:
Show Me the Money!

"It's something very personal, a very important thing. Hell! It's a family motto. Are you ready, Jerry? I wanna make sure you're ready, brother. Here it is: Show me the money. Show! Me! The! Money! Jerry, it is such a pleasure to say that! Say it with me one time, Jerry."

ROD TIDWELL (FICTIONAL CHARACTER FROM THE MOVIE *JERRY MAGUIRE*)

Now that your acquisition toolbox includes a spreadsheet, a rental survey, comparable sales data, proposals from vendors and more, you are ready to talk terms. Although in the real world you will likely have negotiated your purchase price by this time, for the sake of this book and for the sake of your learning, we will discuss it all in one section.

While a significant portion of the investment is actually coming out of your own pocket, the balance will likely be financed, either by a bank or a private lender. To the extent you can, you will want to use the bank's money to improve your financial return on the investment. Once again, my car ride to school as a kid, the story my dad shared with me about OPM. You will see why some investors jokingly refer to this as a drug: OPM (other people's money). OPM should enhance the investment process at all times; at least, it will in a properly structured investment.

The Price is Right

Think of your acquisition as a chain of events that must occur in order to be successful with a particular investment—like you are lining up dominoes to push one and have them all fall down. Since you make your money when you buy, it is important to negotiate the terms in your favor as you enter into the transaction. Although a large portion of this part of the process is going to be market and transaction specific, the fundamentals remain the same. Having become familiar with comparable sales data, you should have a firm grasp on where the market is. And that leads us to a series of questions that you should be able to elaborate on or answer as you determine what price you are prepared to pay.

What is **inventory** like in the marketplace? (Inventory refers to the availability of assets for purchase.)

- Are prices trending upward or downward?
- How does this particular asset fit within my surveys?
- In terms of sales and rental data: Is the income stream superior or inferior to the other comps in your survey? If so, by how much?

As you put your price together, consider your answers to the aforementioned data. Not only is it important for your data to be accurate and precise, it is important to interpret the data truthfully. Another non-financial point to be aware of regarding a sale or transaction is the **ownership scenario**. You should have an understanding of why the particular seller is selling and be aware of any non-monetary terms that will be available. Or, maybe the asset fell into foreclosure and was sold in receivership. Perhaps the seller is having financial troubles and wants to sell, or maybe the seller is conducting a 1031 Tax Deferred Exchange and will need your cooperation with some of their time constraints.

It is also significant, albeit somewhat commonsensical, to uncover how much the seller owes on a property or for how much they are into the property. This can help to understand some of the more psychological components to the negotiation process. You can never know too much about a seller during the process. A good broker will not breach his fiduciary duty but will assist in the process of informing you of soft points or concerns of the seller. Pay attention. Meeting these points will give you a better shot at acquiring the property on your terms.

See, just like with the purchase of a home, if you are looking to get your price, you will likely have to give up the right to choose services: title insurance and escrow. But if you get your number, it is well worth it. Right? I've closed dozens of escrows, and regardless of my personal preference or relationship with a particular escrow officer, if it means getting the deal or not, guess what? We are going with the seller's choice. Remember that. It is almost entirely about money, but not always. These smaller, less significant and non-monetary terms help to grease the wheels. Now, preparing your offer is the next step, so let's get going.

The next tool that you will add to your investment toolbox is the **LOI** or **Letter of Intent**. A letter of intent is a non-binding term sheet that allows you to convey your proposed deal points to the seller and their agent quickly and clearly. The LOI will outline your purchase price, describing the cash you are putting down, the amount you are borrowing, the close of escrow, any contingencies that you will require and the services that you are requesting. Once you finalize the terms, or negotiate back and forth via LOI, you can transcribe the terms on to a purchase agreement, have your attorney draft an agreement or have your agent prepare the offer on your behalf.

Understand that the purchase price should be based not only on the comparable sales data and not only on the income stream, but also on what the property will actually appraise for, or more specifically: how much the bank will loan you on a specific piece of property. Knowing those details and knowing all other terms, you are ready to present. I cannot tell you how much to put down or how much to offer. But I would encourage you to ensure that your investment measures jive with your cost measures at your offer price. So, give yourself some wiggle room and make your move.

Something Borrowed, Something New

And now, the moment we have all been waiting for: It's loan time! It sounds so cool, right? NOT. Some things in life are just unpleasant. Root canals, depositions, picking up dog poop, you get it. Due to the increasing level of financial regulation in this country, applying for and qualifying for a loan is quickly working its way on to the list. However, it is a very necessary part of the business, and it is an imperative piece of the real estate investment puzzle. So, let's get started.

When you are looking for financing, you have two primary sources. You can either go through a **mortgage broker** and spend more, but have more options, or, you can go directly through the **commercial term lending department** of a bank. Going direct through a bank will often provide you with fewer options, but will cost you less in fees and will likely result in cheaper money. Before you commit to either, do your research and inquire with both sources about their best terms and most attractive financing options. Ensure that they will fund the type of loan you are seeking. Show them the LOI that you are working on, and solicit their input. Here, too, you will be able to determine who has a better grasp on financing for your acquisition. Ask about some of their recent fundings or closings, how long it took them, how the appraisals came in in relation to the purchase price of the property and ask about the fees that they will be charging you.

This is about as much pre-marriage dating as you will need before you decide whether or not you are ready to commit, whether you are ready for marriage. As you commit, you will want to know how much of a loan you will be able to get on a particular property and the financing terms, including: interest rate, pre-payment penalties, amortization period and any other details that could affect the marketability of the property should you decide to sell.

Once you receive the proposed terms from your lender, plug the numbers into the underwriting spreadsheet that you previously populated with your cost and investment measures. Based on the numbers, you will be able to determine which option works best for your investment and, more importantly, whether you will benefit from the use of OPM or if you are better off approaching the transaction from a cash perspective.

As we previously discussed, one of the best ways to identify quickly whether or not you will benefit from leverage or the use of other people's money to your benefit is to compare the interest rate on the borrowed money to the capitalization rate of the asset that you are underwriting. If the capitalization rate is higher than the interest rate on the loan that you are considering, then borrowing money will enhance the investment process. If it is not, you will benefit more from investing more of your own cash in the asset.

Think long and hard about your strategy. Unless interest rates are unusually high due to government meddling and or over-regulation, you may want to consider another opportunity. You should always strive to use OPM to your advantage. Make leverage work for you.

It is important to understand and arrive at the most favorable financing terms for your investment. The periodic debt service, both monthly and annually, will have a significant impact on your cash flow and on the overall profitability on your investment. The relationship between

Income and Cash Flow is separated only by debt service. Remember the relationship we previously discussed? From the Gross Income or Total Effective Income, we subtract any and all operating expenses to arrive at the Net Operating Income. From the Net Operating Income, we subtract the payments made to the bank, also known as the Annual Debt Service. Now, we have the Before-Tax Cash Flow. This is your spendable income.

The greater your BTCF, the higher the Cash-on-Cash Rate of Return ($/$%) and the more money in your pocket for additional investments or lifestyle expenses. This cash-on-cash rate of return can be compared to the returns provided by additional asset classes to ascertain which asset class is providing you with a stronger return on investment. And as you can see from the line-item progression, the annual debt service comes between your building and your bank account. Make that barrier thinner than thicker.

Next Steps

Depending on the scenario, you might get a counter offer to your LOI or your offer may be accepted outright. In any case, you will soon embark on a series of financial underwriting tasks. While you are doing your own financial due diligence, the bank will do their own underwriting. Known as the **appraisal process**, the bank will send out an independent expert to study the market just as you have recently done. While they will do this work independently of you and without your input, you are wise to ask for access to information or even for a copy of the completed appraisal.

During the appraisal process, the bank will want to see copies of lease agreements, rent increases and the trailing three years of operational data, including the income and expense data. You will need to identify any capital improvements to explain potentially high maintenance costs. As you review the documents, it is important to look for any operational red flags. Were there period of steep declines in income? Are the security deposits accurately reflected in the banking data, and do they correspond to what is written on paper?

One of the more frustrating aspects of acquiring income property is dealing with an appraiser who may or may not know the market or sub-market. Yes, you will come across appraisers who could not tell you the difference between X and Y, but nonetheless are including them in their valuation of the subject property. For this reason, it is always a good idea to offer the appraiser a copy of your rental and market survey. You want the property to appraise so that you can proceed with your investment. Do not mistakenly believe that the ap-praiser knows best, knows the market or even knows what the prop-erty is worth. He is a scientist conducting an experiment, and without the proper variables, this experiment will be unsuccessful. Offer your assistance, offer your input, and do not hesitate to hammer your lender to get it right. If the appraiser is missing the boat entirely, let your lender know and make sure that the appraiser does not get any more of their business. The lender, like you, wants the deal to get done.

OK, one more thing before I'm done with appraisers. Earlier this year, I had an appraisal done on a property where the street address was in the 900 East block, and the appraiser pulled comps on the 900 West block. This is in a different part of the city, one with lower rents and lower property values. Needless to say, after our meeting he went back and did his homework.

Although the work appears to be painstakingly difficult or complex, on a smaller property the work is really not difficult; it is more about attention to detail. Of course, if you have difficulty working with numbers and are just not a math person, you may want to bring in an expert. That expert could be either a "numbers" person whom you respect or an accountant. Now, on a large scale or a more sophisticated transaction, you may want to consider having an accountant help pick apart the operating information, income statement and or the profit-and-loss statement. While you will have to pay for it, the professional fees you will pay an accountant to audit the financials will prove far less costly than investing hundreds of thousands of your own dollars into a crappy asset and being angry with yourself for a long time.

So, just like things need to check out physically, they need also pass your financial assessment. But remember, it is not entirely about the current or previous income stream. Part of being an astute investor is being aware of upside potential within the marketplace and more specifically how it relates to a specific asset. True, an asset's previous performance will have an impact on the ability to appraise and or receive financing, knowing that the rents are below market or that there is a project coming online that will dramatically change the neighborhood or sub-market is an important part of your financial due diligence. This will allow you to better plead your case for financing or even pursue additional financing, such as bridge financing or other interim financing to help close the gap between the present and future.

Putting It All Together

During the physical due diligence process, you received proposals from vendors that gave you an idea of what it would cost to cure some of the significant issues at the property. Do not expect a seller to fund your upgrades. If they have owned the building for 30 years and have been able to make money without having installed granite countertops and custom cabinetry, it is not likely they will fund your cosmetic enhancement. However, if your physical due diligence uncovered some issues or deficiencies with the key elements of the property, you should address these issues.

So long as you are within your contingency window, approach the seller or their agent with the dollar amount you are looking for in terms of a concession. If there are problems with the roof, termite damage, plumbing issues, faulty wiring, issues with the asphalt and or any items that may or may not be up to code, it is important to address these items with the seller. Not only will doing this show them that you are a serious buyer, but it will also make them aware of potential deficiencies that will likely come up if the deal falls apart and another buyer enters into the picture. You are essentially showing the seller why you would like the purchase price adjusted in your favor and showing him that you know what is important. You are not asking for new carpet or interior paint. Make it easy and convenient for the owner to sell you the building. Do not be the type of buyer who creates obstacles that do not in fact exact. This is a sickness known in the real estate world as "cold feet." If you start to hallucinate or expect the seller to fund your improvements, you need to check your expectations or consider looking in undesirable markets for failed tract-home developments that never sold. Developers could be more willing to work with and accommodate your foolish requests. Multifamily or commercial real estate owners, on the other hand, will not.

Another thing that I like to encourage investors to do, especially when acquiring an apartment building, is to be considerate of the residents of the building that they are purchasing. You see, even though this is your hard-earned equity and in fact a significant investment on your part, you should be mindful of the fact that these are hard-working people who might work nights or have outside issues impacting their personal lives. They do not want to be inconvenienced by continuous visits, inspections and tours of the property. True, you have a job to do, but be considerate. Plan out your inspections and try to coordinate with the appraisal so that you can get it all done at once. Not only will this make it easy on the seller or the seller's management company, it will get you off on the right foot with your soon-to-be residents.

Going back to your acquisition, now that you have negotiated your price, obtained your financing, revisited the purchase price and renegotiated based on any significant issues, you are ready to proceed with your purchase. Successfully obtaining financing can be one of the most significant obstacles that you face during the acquisition process. So long as the appraisal comes in and the bank does not see any issues with occupancy, expense issues or other hazards posing an obstacle, your loan should be approved. In most markets, the loan process can take between four and six weeks, but it is not unheard of to take longer. If traditional financing does not work for one of the aforementioned issues, you can also pursue short-term financing such as a bridge loan or swing loan. However, these loans come at a cost (pun intended) and can often sit at 3 to 4 percentage points above the market interest rates at that point in time, so proceed with caution.

INVESTOR PROFILE

Name: Gary

Prior Occupation: Software Developer

Started Investing at Age: 30

First Investment: Partnered in a 51 Unit apartment complex

Current Real Estate Holdings: Partner in over 600 apartment units

Why Real Estate: More predictable and much less volatility than the stock market. Not to mention, real estate is a physical asset that you can visit.

I Wish I Knew When I Started That: I should not have waited so long and should not have waited to do it on my own. Had I realized earlier on that I had the ability to partner with other like-minded investors to acquire properties, I would not have missed out on some of the best times to acquire commercial real estate within my lifetime.

What I Look For in an Investment: Solid location with the ability to control the property without a lot of influence from neighboring properties that could potentially drag down property values.

To Those Starting Out, I Say: Learn the business and get to know the players within the marketplace. Specialize in a product type or sub-market and know it like the back of your hand. Know the rental rates, sales prices and market values. Know how the market works Focus on the items within your expertise and earn money!

CHAPTER 7:

Strategy and Negotiation

*"Who asks whether the enemy were
defeated by strategy or valor?"*

VIRGIL

One of the most important steps in the acquisition process is the
negotiation of your purchase price and terms. Ideal price and terms
are the difference between a great deal and a good deal, market price
or a discount. Part of successful negotiation requires the buyer to
pose the scenario that best suits him or her to the seller and convince
the seller that this is the strongest, most-acceptable offer that they
will receive. Depending on the personalities involved, this can be
extremely simple or increasingly complicated. As with any type of
negotiation, it is important to check your emotions at the door. This
is about money, not your mood. Do not let your emotions carry over
into the investment process or you will be unsuccessful each and every
time. Besides, emotions are for residential real estate, right? OK, are
you ready? Let's go.

From your very first telephone call to the broker or to the agent, you
need to portray yourself as a serious buyer, an investor who is looking
to amass his or her portfolio. To make an effective first impression, it is
all about asking the right questions. These questions will seem pedestrian because in fact they are. By asking these questions, you will
uncover more details and you will be able to utilize this information

when you are ready to formulate your offer to purchase the property. With that in mind, let's go!

So...Why're You Selling This Fine Building?

Just as people invest in real estate for a number of reasons, people also sell for a number of reasons. Perhaps they are going through a divorce and have to sell. Maybe they need money and don't care about price so long as they get the money quickly. Or maybe, they are trying to sell at the top of the market and don't realize that their market price is a pipe dream. You name it and it could be a reason that a property owner will their property. But you will not know until you ask. So ask! One of your first questions should always be: who is the owner and why are they selling? If the broker is vague and fails to elaborate, rephrase the question. Continue to question the agent until you get the answer that you are seeking.

Now that you have the who and why answered, you are ready to find out about another key motivator: timing. Start gently by asking how long the property has been on the market and then ask about the seller's motivation on timing. That might not be clear, so I'll explain it by giving an example in the sample dialogue below:

> *Buyer:* So, how long has the property been on the market?
>
> *Agent:* 5 months.
>
> *Buyer:* It's been on the market for half a year? How has the seller responded to that? I'd imagine he wants a quick close.
>
> *Agent:* Yeah. Does tomorrow work?

Not only are you building a rapport with the agent, but you are also demonstrating to him that you are asking the right questions and should be perceived as a serious, legitimate buyer. But back to the scenario, you gently eased into whether or not a quick close of escrow is of interest to the seller. If it is, you know that you might have a little wiggle room when it comes to purchase price. Your relationship with the Seller's broker has a significant impact on whether or not your offer will get considered, let alone accepted. If you act like a dope or a putz, your offer will find its way to the circular filing cabinet, also known as the trash bin. Unsure of how much wiggle room the seller might have between his asking price and his bottom line? Don't worry; we will get very direct when it comes to negotiating the right price.

What Has She Done For You Lately?

She being the property, of course. Operations are a key issue when it comes to owning investment real estate. Periods of high vacancy or high maintenance can devastate an owner who is too highly lever-aged and lives solely off of the cash flow. As a result, it is important to understand how the property is performing for the seller. Are there operational issues at present? Is there vacant space that is sitting? These issues can sometimes cause a seller simply to give up. And once a seller has given up, it is time for the buyer to get in. Here's why.

Do you remember how as a kid your parents would get so frustrated with you that even though they didn't want you to do something, they would relent and you would get your way? Well, this is the same logic, only in adulthood. A property performs poorly, on-site management does a terrible job, property management is not up to snuff, etc. While these are issues that you can step in and cure, they are issues that can cause some owners to simply throw up their hands and shout exple-tives. Make this work to your advantage. If your price is not insulting and you happen to time it right, you could be perceived as the White Knight who has arrived to save the seller from his or her financial difficulties. Talk about a win-win situation for everyone.

Now, it is important to understand how much the seller owes on the property so that you understand their actual cash (equity) position and realize whether they are going to be pocketing hundreds of thousands of dollars or taking a haircut on the deal. Knowledge is power, so do your homework. You should also have a firm understanding of how the owner has improved the property. Has he or she continuously invested in the upkeep and maintenance of the property? Or was the last investment the down payment? If the seller's agent is unwilling to share this data, call your title rep and have them find out for you. The information is free, and it is out there. You should also understand whether the seller has any type of pre-payment penalty or acceleration clause in their loan that will cause some exorbitant amount of money to come due upon sale. Failure to do so can result in a costly legal battle, irritation and ultimately, a severely delayed closing of escrow. Always do your research up front so that things don't come back to get you.

Self-Perception Misconception

We've all known people who thought more of themselves than we do. That happens to real estate owners, too, except with real estate owners it's not self-perception—it's property-value perception. Nothing is more frustrating than dealing with an unreasonable or unrealistic seller. So, find out ahead of time with whom you are dealing. Unfortunately, big prices can often result in big egos. If you feel the price is somewhat high for the area, talk to the broker about it. One of my favorite questions to ask a broker is, "Who picked the price?" If the broker admits to picking the price, you can inquire about their logic and ask for comparable sales data to utilize in making your decision. If the seller picked the price, you will most likely find out a lot more about the seller than you cared to know. In one case, I asked this question and the broker launched into a tirade about how the seller was unreasonable, pompous and ignorant. There were other deals out there, so I passed. Ain't nobody got time for that!

Knowing whether the seller has realistic expectations is important. Unrealistic expectations can often keep a deal from happening. Make sure you understand with whom you are dealing and the financial savvy or financial position of the seller.

Presentation & The Power of Appearances

Successful negotiation means coming from a position of power. Remember, you do not have to do anything. You are not being forced to invest in real estate. There is only one person in charge of your investment destiny, and that person is you. Carry this with you as you start to negotiate with the property owner and broker. Since you have already let the broker know that you are serious and you are informed, the next step in solidifying your appearance or stature is through your letter of intent or offer to purchase.

Mask your emotions. Regardless of how bad you want to acquire a particular piece of property, do not show your emotions. Show your interest, but do not overemphasize your feelings or your interest. Unfortunately, the difference between showing your emotions and or keeping a cool poker face can be tens, if not hundreds of thousands, of dollars. A great strategy to utilize in uncovering the seller's motivation is simply to ask questions, but seem indifferent regardless of the broker's response. Of course, you want the broker and seller to like you, but you do not want them to think of you as a sucker on which they are going jack up the price. Let them do that to the sucker who didn't buy and read this book first—not you!

Putting It All Together

So you have now talked to the broker and you know where the owner stands on each of the deal points, it is time to make a deal! There are a number of different strategies suggesting where to start in terms of price. Some say 5%, 10% or even 20%. Each of those statistics is appropriate in the right circumstance. Did that sound vague and ambiguous? Good. It was supposed to be. You see, so much about pricing and terms is market specific, so we will focus less on the exact details and more on strategy.

You want the seller to get in the habit of saying yes or agreeing to the terms that you have proposed, so when I draw out an LOI, I usually put price on the last page, immediately beneath the financing terms and down payment. I spend the first page getting them to agree with me. That is, I get them to like the short escrow, the split escrow fees, their choice in services, their paying my title, me asking only for section 1 termite, etc, etc. If this were boxing, we would be setting them up on the first page with the jab, long left hands that will keep them at bay. Turn the page and BOOM! Here comes the straight right and left hook.

I like to include comparable sales data along with my price if it is off by a significant amount. It is also important to convince the broker why you are the right buyer and why you feel this price is adequate and why the seller should accept it. You will always want to present your offer in person if possible, but when it is not, you need the broker to be able to fight for you. And if the broker believes in your offer and thinks that you are serious enough buyer, he or she will.

Although market specific, I prefer to negotiate back and forth via LOI as opposed to using a purchase agreement. However, if time is of the essence and there are multiple interested parties, you can always try to come to a verbal agreement over the telephone or written over email and then draft an offer to present. This way, the contract is binding once signed and delivered.

The negotiation process is fairly simple but it can take time. Be prepared to go back and forth several times and consider moving or giving in on some of your terms to get close to what matters to you most. Just like in any negotiation, it is a give-take process. So be prepared let go of some of your protection measures such as contingency periods or even specific contingencies to get away with putting less of a deposit down or for offering a lower purchase price.

Some of the more common points of contention or bargaining points are as follows:

- initial deposit forfeiture
- contingencies/contingency periods
- purchase price
- down payment
- duration of escrow

Know that you want your best-case scenario, but come in a little below the best-case scenario so that you have a small window to come up in price or perhaps improve upon the other terms of the transaction. Trust your instincts and do not allow yourself to be bamboozled by a "joker broker" or a "yeller seller." That is, keep a close eye on things, and listen to the stories that you are being told. If you smell a rat, say so. Let things cool off and decide whether or not you want to continue with the transaction. Only you will know whether or not the opportunity is worth pursuing, so trust your judgment. If something seems out of place or too good to be true, chances are, it is.

CHAPTER 8:
Paperwork Means Paper Cuts

"It isn't necessary to imagine the world ending in fire or ice. There are two other possibilities: one is paperwork, and the other is nostalgia."

FRANK ZAPPA

Having already completed your Letter of Intent, Loan Application, Purchase Agreement and a Counter Offer or two, it is now time to put on your auditor's hat and begin the somewhat tedious process of reviewing the plethora of contracts, forms and data associated with your purchase. Be sure to pay attention to the details because the end result could hurt a lot more than a paper cut. So just what is it that you are looking for in the due diligence process? The answer is quite simple: EVERYTHING.

First Things First

Getting ahold of accurate operational data is imperative. While you want to obtain the trailing three years of income statements and expense registries from the current ownership group, you will also want to ask for reports such as the loss/runs from the owner as pertains to insurance coverage, lease agreements and rental increase forms, bank statements, rent rolls and any other transactional-specific forms or documents. Once you have gathered all data, you are ready to proceed.

Perhaps the best place to start your audit is with the lease agreements and or rent increase forms. You will want to request to review each lease agreement and all subsequent rental increase forms to ensure that the rental rates included on the rent roll are in fact current and in effect. In reviewing the contracts and proceeding line by line down the rent roll, you will ensure that the legal contracts held with the tenants are in fact accurate.

As you review the lease agreements, you will want to make note of any promotional, concessional or move-in special type of arrangements they may be noted (or not). For this reason, you will want to refer to bank statements at or around the type of the particular move-in that is in question. For example, a lease agreement might state that a resident pays $1,000-per-month in rent, but upon review, you notice that they moved in with a promotional special that places the resident's effective rent closer to $950 per month. It is important to understand any and all concessions that might be in effect as they have an impact not only on your current rent, but also on your pro-forma goals.

Read through the lease agreements, compare them to the rent roll and note any questions that you might have. You will want to notify the seller of your questions in writing so that you have a chain of correspondence referencing your concerns. This way, if things go south, you will have a written document with response for your reference. While the lease audit or abstract and rent-roll comparison is quite tedious, it is a great tool to use in order to become more familiar with the tenants and any operational issues, such as incomplete lease agreements and or missing documentation. During the due diligence process, you will likely be required to obtain what are known as **"Estoppel Certificates."** If the bank does not require you to obtain Estoppel Certificates signed by the tenants, then you should actively seek them out yourself. Essentially, the estoppel certificate is a document signed off on by the tenant that certifies the terms of the lease agreement related to their tenancy are in fact true. Consider them a very important protective measure.

Without estoppel certificates, a tenant could show up with some sort of concessionary coupon and attempt to pay discounted rent or simply insist that they pay a different amount. And if it cannot be proven, guess who wins? The one with the contract. So get it in writing!

Ensure You're Insured

First of all, understand that the only person who will ever refer to insurance as an investment is your insurance agent. That said, insurance is of the utmost importance; it is just not an investment. Insurance alone will not provide you with a financial reward of any kind. Of course, if something happens at your property and you are adequately covered, then you will more or less be taken care of to the extent the insurance carrier determines necessary. Now, we will discuss insurance coverage more in detail in the WPMS portion of the book, but for the acquisition portion, just know that you will need to get a report known as "loss runs" to your insurance agent. This report summarizes any losses or claims that may have occurred at the subject property in the past. You guessed it: any losses will affect the cost of your coverage and or your insurability, and this will in-turn become an operating expense that has a significant impact on your bottom line.

Once you have your quote, plug the cost into your acquisition spreadsheet. How does the price fit with the previous owner's coverage? Is it comparable? If the coverage is significantly cheaper, check with your agent and ensure that you have sufficient coverage. If it is significantly higher, make sure that you do not have the property over-insured.

The Good, The Bad, The Auditor

Auditing. Detailed review. Sure, it's about as fun as giving blood, but it's also as important as anything you will do in the acquisition process. As you study the income statement, income and expense registries, monitor the month-over-month, year-over-year performance of the property. Compare the bank balances on the accounting reports to the bank statements that correspond to the specific time period you are studying. If you notice any discrepancies or red flags, such as a large line-item expense or perhaps a string of low-collection months in the income portion, highlight it; draw a big, red X in the column; and revisit the report with the seller or the seller's broker.

Again, clarification via email will suffice. It is always good to have the email trail to refer back to if needed. No, I'm not this paranoid in real life—just in business. Besides, no one remembers everything.

More Paper, Less Problems

Now, it wouldn't be a real estate transaction without escrow instructions and loan documents. Sure, you could bypass them in a few special circumstances, but if you are pulling off such sophisticated transactions, then you should write your own book. Always review each and every document in detail. Regardless of the pressure you might feel to move quickly in front of your agent, the escrow officer or a notary public, just slow down and try to read each and every word of each and every line. Understand what you are signing. And if you do not understand, do not sign. As the buyer, you maintain control over the transaction. So outside of your negotiation and contractual obligations, see to it that the terms are correct and that you are comfortable with what has been presented to you to sign.

Specific things to look for include: down payment, contingency periods, commission instructions, wiring information, etc. While it is fairly simple and straightforward if you understand what you are looking for, if you are unaware or concerned that you will make a mistake, then have your attorney review the documents prior to signing. What you are looking for is any typo or misreference, a conflict with a previous agreement or a number transposition. Make sure that the property address is correct and that you are getting everything you asked for and not giving the seller anything that you should not.

By the time your loan is funded, you will look at single-family financing with greater appreciation than ever before. Although technology has helped to simplify things to a certain extent, the lending process from application to funding for multifamily or commercial properties is complex and is littered with supplemental paperwork. Be sure to save everything that you sign, since banks are notorious for misplacing paperwork or requiring you to sign the same paperwork that you signed three days, a week or two-and-a-half weeks ago. Just create a folder in which you will store all of your documents. On almost every loan with which I have been involved, the lender has asked me to re-submit documents that I have already provided them with. So, don't get bothered; just realize that it happens, and keep your eye on the prize.

Reports? Did Somebody Say Reports?

Just like with residential real estate, multifamily and commercial property types require additional reports that a seller cannot necessarily provide. These reports often come through an outside provider. Depending on your market, you might be required to provide a report generated by the City as well. In Los Angeles, we have what is known as a 9-A report. The 9-A report certifies that the structure you are buying is in fact what the city has on file as permitted. I use this as an example only so you are aware of the different reports that could be required.

One thing that I consider a best practice is to visit the City building department within which the property is located. Request a full copy of the building department's file on the piece of real estate that you are looking to acquire. You will soon know more about the property than you ever cared to know. In some cases, you will also know more than the current owner. Yes, that's a good thing. Other reports include an EIR or **Environmental Impact Report**. These are not always required, but can be. If they are required, they can be expensive.

Natural Hazard Disclosures or (NHD) are also important. The NHD will make you aware of any natural issues facing the property. Is it located in a flood zone? Tornado zone? Is it located above an earth-quake fault line? For a measly couple of hundred dollars max, you will soon know all that you need to know about the dirt on which your structure sits. It is a best practice for the seller to pay for this report, but even if they do not, you should buy one for yourself. If you need help, ask escrow or ask your agent to make sure you get a copy.

As you check the paperwork-review line item off of your due dili-gence checklist, realize that you are one step closer to completing the transaction. This is one of the more laborious components of your due diligence, so you should not hesitate to engage an attorney, an accountant or a consultant if you are outside of your comfort level or outside of level of expertise. One of the recurring points that I try to make is that unless you are a professional, there is only so much of the real estate investment process with which you will feel comfortable. And that's fine! Just know when to say when and engage the appropri-ate expert.

INVESTOR PROFILE

Name: Donald

Prior Occupation: Mortician

Started Investing at Age: 10, really, my parents signed the papers!

First Investment: Duplex

Current Real Estate Holdings: 33 units and a partner in other ventures

Why Real Estate: It's the only asset class that I have been successful with.

I Wish I Knew When I Started That: Money can be tough to come by and it is important to save your money so that you can invest it wisely. Just starting out, partners would have really been a help.

What I Look For in an Investment: Has to be on the sunny side of the street. Location is important.

To Those Starting Out, I Say: Buy as much as you can as young as you can. Get a lot when you're young.

CHAPTER 9:

Prepare For Turbulence

"Sometimes when people are under stress, they hate to think. And that's the time when they most need to think."

WILLIAM J. (BILL) CLINTON

You ever notice how the first bit of turbulence that you encounter on a flight prompts the pilot to turn on the "fasten seatbelt" sign? Or maybe if that quick bit of turbulence lasts longer than expected, the pilot will voice over the loudspeaker and reassure passengers not to panic. Well, turbulence can occur when investing in real estate, too, and you need a calm head to handle the bumpy process. Wealth building is not easy and the road to success is a rough, bumpy ride.

For a majority of adults in our capitalistic society, there is one reason we get out of bed at the crack of dawn and head to work: MONEY. And when you focus on or deal with money, people grow emotional. People grow sensitive. People are not who they usually are. Keep this in mind during escrow. It will allow you to hold and maintain the upper hand in the negotiation. So, ensure that you are protected contractually, but remember the "people" component. People are the wild card in any transaction.

However simple it may seem, remind yourself of the need to maintain your composure. You see, the late night phone calls will come. The strategy. The poker-like game playing. It is a part of the business, and you will need to take it in stride in order to succeed. It is not uncommon for a seller to grow remorseful over agreeing to too low of a sales price and asking for more money. In several instances, I have encountered a seller receiving the price they asked for and decide that they no longer want to sell their piece of real estate. With the appropriate contract and terms, you are protected in the event this happens. But even though the "people" component to negotiation is huge, it is not everything. More often than not, it's money that matters.

You see, the bank can come back with appraisal issues asking you to put more money down. And while you want this to happen before you have removed your loan or before the appraisal contingency is removed, it is not always a guarantee. Be ready to make a decision on whether to put down a higher down payment in order to proceed. Unfortunately, I have never had a bank come back and ask for a lower down payment. It just does not happen.

Although this is or can be a highly emotional process, it is important to make things as simple as possible. And that means making level-headed decisions and not acting impulsively. Also, it is important to remember what we previously discussed about appraisers: they are not market specialists or market experts. They are professional report writers who do not know anything about the markets on which they report; they pull data and compile it into a written summary. Would you let a podiatrist deliver your soon-to-be-born child, or would you prefer an obstetrician? Right. You would want the professional, the expert, the individual who knows the ins and outs. So when an appraiser poses his or her opinion on value, it is just that. Don't hang everything on what an appraiser has to say. You are the expert. You know where the value is.

Just like we discussed in the previous chapter, the posturing that you will utilize to get your offer accepted is the same way you should handle yourself during escrow. As things change, it is important to separate the big from the small, the significant from the miniscule.

And through it all, it is important to maintain a level of professionalism that your peers and competitors respect and admire.

One of my favorite metaphors for life is the sport of boxing. In boxing, they always say it's the shot you don't see coming that hurts the most. For that reason, you want to use the quick and heavy shot to your advantage, but be on the defensive for it as well. How can you do this? Simple: bob and weave!

It never ceases to amaze me that someone will invest $250,000 to $1,000,000 of their hard earned money in real estate, but will not spend $2,500 on an attorney to draft and review a purchase agreement that best protects them, or spend a fraction of that cost to review their loan documents on their behalf. I see this as a best practice, not even as a precautionary measure. You see, a contract attorney will agree or disagree with verbiage and try their best to protect YOU as their client. On the other hand, the bank will try to protect itself and will present you with a skewed contract that includes lots of fine print intended to make your life difficult and ensure they get their money. Again, don't be scared; just be aware.

One other thing that you should add to your acquisition toolbox is a blank calendar that covers 30, 45, 60 and 90 days depending on the duration of your escrow. Mark out the key dates such as contingency removals, inspections, when certain documents were received, etc. This will help you as a try to remember bits of information or as you work on the seller for certain credits in escrow, if relevant.

So, what about when you get hit with the straight right? It happens to the best of us. Simply put, it's all about reaction. Rather than jump right up off of the canvas, stay seated and take time to think. Maybe the straight right was finding out that the building needs to be re-plumbed. Or maybe it could be that the building is in need of a new roof, and the seller is not going to budge on price. Well, first things first. Respond by explaining the issue to your agent, getting proposals and seeking the appropriate solution. Here again, you are demonstrating your desire to proceed with the transaction while also doing your best to protect yourself. Once you have compiled the bids and you know how much the job will cost, approach the seller and ask for a credit. Realize that when you have previously agreed to one price and you come back asking for $20,000, $50,000, $75,000 or $250,000, it is not unheard of, but it has the potential to go over like a led zeppelin. Torpedoed. Straight into the ground. However, if you continue to move forward with the transaction, the seller will also transform mentally from the seller to the sold. While you are in fact obtaining proposals on what it will cost to make repairs, the seller is structuring his next transaction. In the process, the seller's mindset will change. Just like you want to buy the building, they want to sell the building. Keep that in mind for negotiation purposes. Timing is everything. Now, hit them with your request.

See, it's not just about deal making, it's about deal closing. Being a big picture thinker and seeing what truly matters can make the difference between acquiring an investment and being stuck in portfolio purgatory, the land where you live in analysis paralysis on the what-ifs and never move forward. If you take one thing from Chapter 8 or Chapter 9 of this book, it should be that you should never let your position on whether to proceed with an investment or not depend on emotions or on feelings. Sound investments are based on facts and factual data, not emotions. Remember that.

The Spreadsheet Stare-Down

*"I think confrontation is healthy because
it clears the air very quickly."*

BILL PARCELLS

A good spreadsheet will help you quickly determine whether or not to proceed with a potential investment opportunity. A great spreadsheet will tell you why you should or should not proceed. Yes, the devil is in the details, so deciding which data should be included in your matrix is of the utmost importance. While you will want to have a complete summary of the investment in its current state, you will also want to include enough pro-forma or potential data to ensure that future projections or growth trends are accounted for in the acquisition. As you know, you are investing not just for current, in-place income, but also for future income stream.

Have you ever had the feeling of winning a big game? Or maybe it is the feeling of securing a big account. Do you know the feeling of excitement that accompanies such success? I have achieved the same thrill with my spreadsheets. Did you notice, I even referred to them as "my spreadsheets"? I wish I were lying, but it's the truth. You see, after spending hours and hours of data entry, cell tweaking, formula creat-ing, number projection, data manipulation and data massaging, you realize that your potential acquisition will work for you. It will meet your goals. There is a feeling of adrenaline or excitement in knowing that the next step is in preparing an offer.

Now, I have also had moments where I want to toss my calculator across the room and leave the office in pain and agony after spending hours on a potential acquisition that did not work. Drama, exaggeration and theatrics aside, let's have a look at the important components of your spreadsheet. Realize that investment and cost measures will differ between asset classes (multifamily, office, retail or industrial), but we will focus primarily on multifamily and office herein.

From Offer Writer to Underwriter

First things first when preparing your spreadsheet, and that means having a detailed accounting of all units or suites included on the potential investment. You will want to account for the unit mix (bed/bath count), the square footage of the individual space and you will also want to account for the current rent received by each of the respective units. For office or retail space, this will include the number of suites, square footages and common area space. Next, you will want to insert some of the details about your offer price and terms. Plug in your proposed purchase price, down payment and then factor in your loan amount, interest rate and the amortization period.

Once you have the basis for your investment, what you might otherwise refer to as the "bones", review the operating expenses and start to plug in the key recurring expenses. Property taxes, maintenance, staffing, insurance, utilities, marketing, landscaping and administrative costs are some of the basics with which you should start. Now, you might remember that earlier on in the book, we discussed how the cap rate was a subjective number because a certain owner might operate the property with higher or lower expenses than another operator. Well, here is your firsthand example. As you review operating expenses, it is important to ensure that your costs are in fact accurate and correct.

Make sure that you are utilizing realistic numbers for property taxes, utilities and insurance. How do you ensure that the numbers are accurate? Call the county, call the utility companies who are involved, and call your insurance agent. Just as the cap rate or operating expenses are subjective, so is your insurance coverage. Make sure that your insurance agent understands and can advise on insurance coverage for the property type that you are interested in acquiring. If not, find someone who is. Oftentimes when underwriting a potential investment, I find that my potential price for insurance will be significantly higher than the current policy in place. Come to find out, it has to do with the level of coverage. Some owners like to keep just the bare minimum required. Don't be THAT owner. Things happen, and you do not want to be left with inadequate coverage in the event of a significant loss. Don't over-insure either. Yes, there is such a thing.

Now that you have plugged your operating expenses into the spreadsheet, realize that the next step is to identify whether any of these numbers is off the mark. Is it high? If so, why? What should the numbers realistically be, and what will it take to get the property to operate in such a fashion? And no, just using a lower number will not solve the problem. Understand the issue and pursue a solution.

Do you need an example? I thought so. OK, so you discover that current maintenance costs were high due to several recurring roof leaks. And rather than replace the roof, the owner has decided to just sell the dang building. Well, you do your homework and find out what it will cost to replace the roof and solve the problem. Sure, it will cost more in the short-term, but you will save over the long-term. As a result, your maintenance expense will be lower, and thus, your cash flow will be higher. Factor the cost of your new roof into your acquisition price, separately and as a capital improvement. You want this expense to weigh in your overall return on investment, not in your ability to obtain financing.

With your current rents, going-in purchase price and financing terms complete, you will now switch gears to focus on future rental trends and market growth. Now, nobody has a crystal ball, but depending on the region, market or sub-market within which you are looking, you will be able to understand recent activity and discover whether the activity has been downward, flat or upward in recent years. Are there new projects that are being built? Is there a new area amenity? Are there new jobs being added to the marketplace that will have an impact on occupancy and rates? Whether the impact is positive or negative, it is important to understand where the trend is headed. It has a significant impact on the continued profitability of your investment. Here, you will want not only to consult your broker for rental rates and trends, but you will want to independently verify these trends as well. Make the telephone calls yourself and log your notes.

On my spreadsheet, I include a low-market and a high-market box for rental rates. The lower rate should be the absolute low: minimal growth. The high should be the best-case scenario. That is, everything goes as hoped and you crush it. Now, if you are paying attention, you will remember that we previously went over the cost and investment measures. Yes, you guessed it. We have our cost measures plugged in, so now we can proceed to analyze and assess whether or not we proceed with this particular investment or move on to the next one.

You are the only person who knows what you are looking for in a real estate investment, or more specifically, your financial situation outside of your real estate portfolio. As such, it is important to have an understanding of your investment goals. Different investors require different returns. For that matter, different investors invest for different reasons. So basic, so redundant and so cliché, but so TRUE. Now, let's say you want all four benefits of owning commercial real estate. We can immediately check off tax shelter and hedge against inflation because we know that any real estate investment will satisfy those requirements. But let's look at equity buildup.

Where are we at within the market? Are prices on a downward slide? Are they in a trough? Are prices on an upward climb? Obnoxious real estate salesman always tell us that the key is to "buy low and sell high," but that is easier said than done. And, as over-simplified as it might sound, it is true. You see, it is impossible to know for certain where you are within the market, but if you study the trailing two to three years of sales and rental data, you can come close. Of course, if I had a crystal ball or could read your fortune, I would not be involved in real estate at this stage of my career. I would have retired years ago. So just be aware. If prices have declined consistently and have flattened out, or, if prices have slowly increased over the past few years or months, then it could also be a good time to purchase for equity buildup. Now, that will not guarantee you cash flow, but as long as you are aware going in, you are OK. Oh, did I mention that cash flow is my favorite benefit? More on this in a minute.

Across the United States, some markets are prone to slow or no growth in terms of market values, due in part to the abundance of land open for future development and the overbuilding that can occur at specific points in the market. So, please understand that this is intended to give you an understanding of what can occur and not a specific direction. It is always important to consider your local trends. So while equity buildup might only be possible over the short term in certain markets, cash flow is possible everywhere depending on how you purchase a piece of property.

For me, cash flow is what makes real estate the best investment. It is what beats stocks, bonds, minerals and other passive income streams. With that, it is important to understand that investing in and owning real estate is more labor intensive than investing in other asset classes. So it is important to receive a return on investment that substantiates not only your financial investment, but also your time and labor investment.

And if you thought the investment process was frustrating, wait until you get to the management portion of the management process. Property management has been known to make people so frustrated and so irritated that they throw in the towel and sell their portfolio. Before you do that, I would encourage you to hire a professional management company. We will discuss how to hire the management company that best fits your method of ownership later on in the WPMS portion of the book. Because cash flow is what real estate is all about. It helps to generate income that in turn supports your lifestyle. Now, back to it.

Depending on how much money you have and whether or not you will self-manage your real estate or hire a property management company to do it for you, you will have a different preference for your return on investment. Of course, you will always want the greatest possible return, but will have different requirements based on your level of involvement. This day in age, it is almost a guarantee that you will beat the return provided by the bank. Meaning, if you left your equity sitting in a bank account, the minimal or laughable return on your investment by the bank-proclaimed "high interest-earning account" will be so minimal that you will not even notice that a return was earned. But is it prudent to just want to beat the bank? That answer is subjective.

For some, the answer is yes. Some people have so much money that they are simply looking to diversify their investment portfolio and earn some type of return on investment. Now, real estate will in most cases beat the bank and will also provide the remaining three of four benefits. But if you are not independently wealthy and are instead looking to invest to boost your income and receive additional passive income, a 1.5% return on investment will not help much. So while the decision will be entirely up to you and made at your discretion, you will want to look for a minimum current or going-in return on investment of 3% with the short-term potential (1.5 to three years out) of 5% + and ultimately the long-term return of greater than 5%. This is possible in many markets nationwide. It is especially possible in the Southern California market of 2013.

Your spreadsheet should demonstrate to you just what the individual measures are. What is a 1.5%, 3%, 5%, 10% return on investment? Can you afford to invest X amount of dollars into an asset and not have immediate access to it? Opponents of real estate investment state that it is illiquid and as such, is inferior to stocks or bonds that can be easily sold. Well, newsflash: real estate can also be sold quickly. You just might not like the price that it will sell for.

Now that you have assembled your spreadsheet, it is up to you to identify and underwrite the properties that are of interest to you. The more properties you underwrite, the more you know the market, the more you become aware with what to look for and the closer you come to making acquisitions and building your portfolio. It can be too easy for the part-time investor to push things off and or wait for another day to underwrite, so be hard on yourself. Set a goal to spend at least one hour each night split as follows. At first, take 15 minutes of searching LoopNet for available opportunities and then spend 45 minutes underwriting. Once you become more familiar with your spreadsheet and learn to identify some of the key triggers that you are looking for, balance out your time and spend the first 30 minutes searching and the second 30 minutes underwriting.

After you have reviewed each possible purchase scenario paired with the corresponding income and expense matrixes, you are ready to make the "go" or "no go" decision. Be forewarned, this can cause fist pumps or foul-mouthed outbursts. Either way, you are all the better for having underwritten and evaluated your potential investment.

Remember the Peter Drucker quote, "What gets measured, gets done." You will be closer to making your acquisition and will be more aware of the marketplace and the opportunities that are out there. And as a result, you will be able to more quickly identify the investment opportunities on which you should move.

INVESTOR PROFILE

Name: Barb

Prior Occupation: Legal Secretary

Started Investing at Age: 47

First Investment: Purchased an 8 Unit Apartment Complex

Current Real Estate Holdings: Owns 37 units across 3 properties

Why Real Estate: At the time, my husband and I were working a lot and had a significant amount of savings as well as expendable income and needed the taxable write-off that real estate can provide.

I Wish I Knew When I Started That: You can do so much on your own and you can truly learn on the job. After a bad experience with a management company, we ended up taking over management duties at our property and did it all ourselves. We joined the apartment association for their resources and started doing it all. We collected rents, did maintenance and leased the units ourselves. This is a great way to build sweat equity and to learn a lot about your properties and the markets in which they are located.

What I Look For in an Investment: Tax shelter was the biggest driving factor for us when in investing in real estate, but as for physical characteristics we looked for ample parking, built post-1979 due to lead based paint and we looked for the worst building on the best street. These simple drivers made us quite successful.

To Those Starting Out, I Say: Be conservative and do not overleverage your investments. Start small and learn on the job. Do more, learn more, question your vendors and learn the "hows" and "whys". Do the work yourself while you can and you will help to keep your expenses lower. Finally, when you're ready to retire, hire a management company.

PART III:

Winning Property Management Strategies

CHAPTER 11:
Winning Property Management Strategies

"The only thing that I am addicted to right now is WINNING!"

CHARLIE SHEEN

Having finally closed your escrow and become the proud owner of income property, it is time to determine whether you are better suited for the path of passive or active ownership. Part of this is a quality of life choice and part of this is just preference. For some people, it is easy to self-manage and the process requires minimal time. For others, the process is increasingly frustrating and complicated. The results? Headaches, deteriorating quality of life and stress. Now, doesn't that contradict the very reasons we invest? OF COURSE! So, be smart.

You see, managing property is not easy to do, but it is easy to do wrong. Just like any other service business, the ability to cater to the humanistic needs and ideals of our customers is at the center of our success. The ability to quickly and efficiently troubleshoot while keeping our customers satisfied is key to high occupancy and even higher profits. Rather than shoot from the hip, strategically plan your course of operation and reach for your goals accordingly. You will realize that in your attempt to become a more hands-on or proactive landlord, your resident relations, your property value and possibly even your rents will improve. Don't believe it? Google me. I know what I am talking about.

Strategizing ahead of time can help to minimize the inevitable pains of management and the very fact that you are reading this book shows that you are concerned. Make sure you carry the same forethought you demonstrated while doing your due diligence and acquisition forward as you operate your property. And while you cannot prevent all problems, you can certainly think ahead and project so that you have the correct system in place to resolve these issues when they do occur. Often times, the biggest mistake that new landlords make is in their approach to management. People think that it's as easy as opening the mailbox and then depositing the rent checks. Truly, that's what most people think before they make their first income property purchase. Allow me to break the news to you: it doesn't quite work that way. At least it doesn't at first.

There will be moments of absolute peace and quiet, moments of joy and moments of hell. Through all you will experience in owning and operating apartments, it is important to remember two things at all times: keep your composure and don't sell. That is, don't grow so frustrated, so irritated with residents or maintenance issues that you lose sight of the reason you own the property: to make money. Your residents have nothing to lose and will try your patience. They are of the "new" American way. That is, they approach each and every business transaction as though they are dealing with a Fortune 500 company that is going to dish out a freebie simply because a customer complains. Society has trained them to think that way, but that's not how we do things. Not now. Not ever.

We fix small problems before they become big problems and big problems before they become huge problems. We take care of maintenance requests the moment we hear about them. And more importantly, we keep our rents high so that our investment maintains its value and generates the strongest possible return. You see, landlords are great people. Slumlords, on the other hand, are not. If you do not recognize the difference or cannot differentiate between the two by now, you might need more help than I can provide in this one book. So call me, I also provide consulting services.

In being a proactive landlord, you will take steps and encourage your residents to behave this way. And through time and behavioral conditioning that would make Pavlov smile, your residents will ultimately submit to your craft. When this occurs, you will know that you are no longer a zookeeper. You are now a landlord. But how do we get there? How do we evolve from zookeeper or slumlord to landlord? The road is paved with customer service and TLC not just for your property, but for your tenants as well. Follow me as we explore this transition from good to great, from average to excellent.

CHAPTER 12

As We Continue On

*"Do you want to know who you are? Act, don't ask!
Action will delineate and define you!"*

THOMAS JEFFERSON

From the moment you decide to invest, your quest to secure and develop wealth through real estate has begun. And with this book in your hands or on the screen of your e-reader, you are already taking the right steps. In this chapter, we will discuss some of the items that you should accomplish prior to closing escrow on your income-producing property. While some items can be done at any time, some can and should be completed during the escrow period. Yes, the loan and due diligence process can take longer during the acquisition of income property than during the purchase of residential property, so you will have plenty of time to prepare for ownership.

Simple planning will go a long way. And you should realize that there is a direct correlation between your effort and your return on investment. The more you care for your property and the more diligent you are in managing it, the greater the potential income. This is a fairly simple principle that is often forgotten or overlooked by landlords. Success is not an accident, and you will not simply fall into it. With that, let's examine the first few steps towards your success.

Mental Preparation

Thomas Jefferson once proclaimed that "all men are created equal," but it is important to understand going into your real estate venture that not all men think alike. While you might be honest and straightforward, it is likely that during your course of property ownership you will unfortunately have to deal with someone who is dishonest, untruthful or otherwise an opportunist looking to capitalize on a mistake or unfortunate circumstance. This could be a resident, it could be a vendor or even an employee. Although you cannot control the actions of others, you can certainly take steps to minimize risk and also prepare yourself for the inevitable because it will happen.

Just like the 1980s brought us the art of positive self-affirmation and the idea that mental conditioning would bring us success, you can help to minimize future stresses by simply understanding that you will one day be taken advantage of, lied to or threatened by a resident or vendor. This can even result in costly legal battles. Know this and proceed with caution. Keep an eye out for trouble, and always be aware.

Take steps to minimize potential liabilities by keeping exceptional records, staying in tune with the physical condition of the interior and exterior condition of your property and by staying up to date with the legalities of doing business in your area. And again, even though you do all of this while maintaining professionalism, you can still be accused, sued or threatened. Do not let this dissuade you or deter you from making what is arguably one of the best investments a person can make: purchasing apartments. Office properties can be a sound investment as well, but as a property-type it is more susceptible to economic conditions. When things get bad, people close their businesses and vacate their office space, but they still need a place to live. Remember that!

We will later discuss insurance coverage, the various policies that you should hold as a property owner and how they can help to protect you. Even so, it is important to imbed in your brain that you have zero control over the actions of others. But, those actions do have consequences, and you can suffer the repercussions of their poor decisions. So be prepared mentally and be proactive.

Association Participation

One of the most important things you can do to protect yourself and your investment is much cheaper than insurance. Joining your local apartment association or property-rights organization will help you not only in managing your property, but also in keeping you up-to-date on pending legislation, new laws, rules and regulations as they relate to your property. Oh, and did I mention: it will help protect your rights as a property owner. One of the best things about these groups or associations is that they will often have their own **lease agreements**, **disclosures** and other forms that you can utilize in assembling your own lease agreement for your property. This can help to save you time and money in legal fees that would be spent preparing one for your own property.

Oftentimes, when you buy a new property, you will find that the previous owner wrote his lease agreements on a paper towel, the back of a napkin, a McDonald's bag that has been ripped down the seam and undone. You name it, I've seen it. Don't be that guy. Imagine holding up a McDonald's bag in court, trying to gain the respect of the judge. Imagine your argument:

> "Well Your Honor, somewhere beneath the grease stain
>   and the ketchup splotch she signed the fixed-term lease,
>   but you can't see it now."
> – Losing Landlord

Case closed: You're an idiot, and it's amazing that someone so stupid can own property. So, join the association, go to the meetings and utilize their forms. It's a minimal cost, usually based on the number of rental units you own. For the service and support, networking and knowledge that you will receive, the nominal membership fee is well worth it. Pay it and be on your way to success.

Build Your Team

Aligning yourself with reputable and responsible professionals will not only make your job easier, but it can also save you money. Depending on your property and its location, you will need service providers on a one-off or continuous basis. Some typical vendors include: plumbers, handymen, carpet and flooring installers, cleaning crew, emergency-service providers, painters, landscapers and pest control. You will want to have price lists, insurance certificates and updated contact information on at least three of each vendor handy in a three-ring binder or otherwise available all the time. They should name you, your company and the property as additionally insured on their policies. Before you allow someone to do work on your property, they must provide for you the appropriate licenses and insurance. Failure to require this is just too much of a risk. Don't do it.

Soon, you will realize that these vendors will become your lifeline. They can come in to provide expertise and help troubleshoot maintenance issues, or they can rush to finish a job on short notice because you have taken an extra effort to establish a bond. Take the time to build a relationship ahead of time. It will pay off. In fact, these vendors can help you during the due-diligence process as well. Ask them to assist during the physical inspection of your potential acquisition. You will gain their insight and expertise into the overall condition of the property as it relates to the trade. This can greatly assist in establishing price points of repairs, or better yet, the amount you should ask for in escrow.

To use a baseball analogy, a good, strong, well-maintained vendor list is like your bullpen. You will need to have a number of options available depending on the situation in which you are involved. When the time is right, you need to be able to contact and count on your vendor to get the job done in a timely, cost-effective manner. Do your homework and your research ahead of time to arrive at your rotation so that you do not get stuck.

Fair Housing Training

Exercise equality in your operation of rental housing. Treat everyone equally and be the same owner/manager to resident A as resident B or resident JJJ. Most importantly, regardless of their personal circumstances or the award-winning sob stories that you will hear, you should show no preferential treatment to anyone. As basic and unsophisticated as this may sound, if you follow this simple principle from the get-go, you will be fine.

Few things are more devastating to a property owner than a fair-housing claim or lawsuit. Even if the landlord ends up winning the case, it can still cost tens of thousands, if not hundreds of thousands, in legal defense fees and can sincerely compromise your quality of life. Worse yet, none of those defense fees will be reimbursed to the owner. So, keep your nose clean and follow the law. Not sure what the law is? Well, since you became a member of your apartment association, you have access to their fair-housing resources. Often, you can attend local fair-housing training for a minimal fee. Attend these classes, befriend the instructors and soak up what you hear. For a half-day seminar, once per year, you can do yourself a lot of good.

Landlord/tenant law firms also offer these courses, and that might be an option for you if you will be putting a number of people through a course or would like special care and attention. Unfortunately, people view fair housing in a negative light at times because of the unwarranted threats that angry tenants can use in conjunction with the organization. Case in point: tenant doesn't pay rent and doesn't make arrangements to pay, gets served with a three-day notice to pay or quit, doesn't pay or quit, gets sent to attorney to commence eviction and suddenly, the landlord is accused of discriminating against this tenant, and the tenant threatens to "call Fair Housing."

As proactive landlords, we welcome these calls because we know that we are not in the wrong. Follow the rules, treat all current/prospective residents equally, and you will be fine. And just so you know, one of the first questions that Fair Housing will ask the complaining party is… You guessed it: Have you paid your rent yet?

Bankers & Attorneys

You thought having a good serviceperson was important? Well, your business, legal and financial resources are even more important. They are absolutely imperative to your success.

You will want to have both a friendly and cooperative business bank for your income property and a landlord/tenant attorney that will not only evict and defend, but answer the many questions you will come across on a daily basis. Good landlord/tenant or business law firms will provide the Q & A to their clients as a gratuity. Find it and take advantage of it. Unsure of where to find a good business bank or a solid landlord/tenant attorney? Check the association's list or their magazine. They will have more than a few for you to consider.

The Money

"Neither a borrower nor a lender be."

— Polonius, Shakespeare's *Hamlet*

Banking is such a simple thing. You put money in and take money out. But you, the property owner, who rarely bounces checks and does not overdraw your account, are much different than your overdrawn and cash-strapped clientele, who will bounce checks, know they bounced checks and wait until you receive your statement to issue payment. This is not how we are going to do things. We are proactive thinkers, which means that since we have shaken hands, shared stories and sipped coffee together, our bank is going to call us the instant the check comes back and tell us who bounced the check. This way, we have all the necessary information and can respond at once.

These relationships are easier had with smaller, regional banks. Although business-banking services are provided by all of the top dogs, big four included, you will find a more personalized approach taken at the smaller institution. Of course, in our current economic times you will want to be sure that the institution is FDIC insured and otherwise solvent.

Your business-banking relationship can also be the springboard for exceptional, relationship-based lending opportunities. Local banks are often interested in gaining all of their customers' business, and as a result, will offer discounted rates and or preferential treatment to those looking to obtain either financing for new acquisitions or refinancing. Friends of all kinds are important, especially those with money. Be sure to make friends at the bank; it will pay off (pun intended).

Legal Eagles

Starting out in management, you will want to explore a number of scenarios. While I am not an attorney and cannot provide you with legal advice, I can tell you who you should talk to and what type of attorneys you should have on speed dial.

From the moment you invest, you will want to have an **estate-planning attorney** ensure that you are holding title in the most beneficial method of ownership possible. There are a number of tax breaks achievable through sophisticated estate planning. Ask your trusted friends and colleagues whom they work with and have heard good things about, and find your expert. Either before or once you own the property, you will want to have some sort of ownership entity established to limit your personal liability should tenants sue, an injury occur or some other unforeseen circumstance. Here you will want to have a business attorney on your side.

Once you own the property you will want a **landlord/tenant attorney**. Landlord/tenant matters are so complex and so frequently changing in California that often judges will excuse themselves from a small-claims case or eviction case if they are not an expert. When this happens and a judge pro-tem takes over, landlords are often surprised to learn that this new judge is actually a landlord/tenant attorney or otherwise an expert. And there is nothing that one of these attorneys hates more than seeing an unprepared or unequipped landlord.

You are not this guy. Because…

As we discussed in the first step of management, you have joined the apartment association. In joining the association, you frequently read their trade publications and attend their seminars to stay educated and informed. In doing so, you have taken advantage of the networking opportunities available to you. As such, you have met with and know of at least three landlord/ tenant attorneys. Establish an agreement with your favorite of the three landlord/tenant attorneys where you can contact them for day-to-day issues and other questions that will come up during the course of your business in exchange for all of your eviction and/or collections business.

You will soon see that this relationship is well worth the trouble. In today's day and age, with technology and the abundance of information made available on the Internet, you will likely find your customers questioning you or relaying to you advice that they have misinterpreted. Being able to pick up the phone and consult your attorney with a routine question will relieve many a headache.

If you employ any resident managers or maintenance personnel, you will also want to have a solid **employment-law attorney** with whom you can consult with on the many issues that will come up during the course of business. This is especially relevant in California, where business owners have few rights, other than to pay exorbitantly high amounts of taxes, incur all the liability and then get taxed again.

Insurance

Insurance and the many types of coverage available to landlords can vary by the location and size of the property. Typical policies you should consider include: property, crime, general and other liability, workman's comp and employers liability insurance. Your lender may have specific requirements, and again, you might have other coverage required by your area. As an example, in California coverage for earthquakes and or flooding can be required depending on the location of a property.

As you operate your property, you will notice that insurance can be a significant expense, and it correlates to the size of your property—

meaning the bigger the property, the larger the expense. That said, it is important for you to establish a network of at least three **insurance brokers** working with different carriers to competitively bid and assess your insurance needs. Realize that there is always too little or not enough, but you do not need to over-insure. In a perfect world, and if cost were no object, you would obtain the maximum levels of coverage possible. However, there is a happy, cost-effective medium that should protect you and your interests.

Be sure to consult with licensed insurance professionals in evaluating the necessary coverage, and pick the one that best protects you without breaking your budget. Budget? Yes. We will get to that.

Communicate and Correspond

With your support team assembled, you will now want to establish a method by which to communicate and correspond. For mailing purposes, a post-office box is your best bet. For in-person business not dealt with at the property, only if you are opposed to meeting at the property, you should arrange for some sort of office environment. Home addresses are never a good idea. So if possible, utilize your work address, or, if it is in your budget, rent a small office to house your records, facilitate tenant meetings and receive mail.

Rather than use a landline, purchase a cellular phone with an inexpensive calling plan. Use this phone and only this phone in your leasing, management and correspondence. Failure to do so will result in unwanted calls to your home or personal telephone on a consistent basis. Do not make this mistake because they will call you. They will not use the line that you ask them to call on if they have your cellular phone number, so do not give them the opportunity to bother you. Use a cellular phone and record a greeting that informs your residents or prospects of what to do during an emergency and when you typically return phone calls. This will help you maintain your sanity. You are not a robot and you are not expected to be available 24/7. Tenants who think you need to be reachable 24/7 are sadly mistaken.

Making the Introduction

Having completed the necessary prep work, established the systems and assembled your team, you are now ready to become the landlord.

Drumroll please …

It is important to introduce yourself to your tenants and establish yourself as a kind and caring, yet firm and steadfast individual. Like we discussed in the fair housing portion, do not show bias and always be sure to treat everyone equally. To introduce yourself, start by writing a friendly letter, notifying your residents that you are the new landlord. Give them addresses and numbers for correspondence, and make an attempt to reach them on a personal level. Realize that you, yes you, are now the recipient of what is likely their biggest personal expense each month. You represent the biggest check they cut. So yes, your being a likeable person makes that check easier for the tenant to cut.

After distributing the letter, there are a number of inexpensive things that you can do to further your rapport with your residents: hosting some sort of a barbeque, having pizzas delivered, gift cards as introductory pleasantries, etc. There are many things that can be done out of appreciation for your paying customers. With so many nice, affordable things that can be done to foster a good relationship, why wouldn't you? Don't be lazy. Do it. Realize that you will likely be the first person to do this for them. It will leave a memorable impression on them, and they will remember it come the first of the month when rent is due.

As you meet your residents, be sure to account for the people you are meeting and where they live. It is always a good idea to cross-verify that the information you have been given from the previous owner or landlord matches up. You might find that some apartments are like the famous clown car at the circus—you know, the car that seems so small but somehow fits 18 or 19 clowns inside? Yes, this can happen, especially when there is no on-site manager. So keep an eye out and be sure to take notes.

Essentially, what you are trying to do is establish a personal bond, while still maintaining a professional relationship. You are not their friend. You are their landlord. You are kind and caring, pleasant and attentive, but you have a job to do and a service to provide. Do it, and do not blur the lines.

Think Streamline

As you know, one of the recurring themes of this book is forethought and planning. People do not become millionaires or multi-millionaires without first strategizing. So do what the wealthy people do. Think things through. How does this fit within the chapter? Easy. As you prepare to transition from buyer to owner, make sure that you have collected the pertinent information and that you have on hand the necessary documents to ensure a hiccup-free change in ownership. This means that you will want to gather a host of documents listed below, as well as the necessary account numbers and contact information to ensure a timely transfer of utility services into your name. Failure to coordinate ahead of time can result in ... you guessed it: billing problems, lots of time on hold and worse yet, unannounced shutoff of utilities or disruption of service. It is much easier to make a phone call or send an email ahead of time.

Documents

Immediately upon closing escrow, you will want to pick up the original copies of all leases, applications and any other pertinent operating information related to the property. Any blueprints, plans, drawings, sketches, schematics, applications, leases, invoices, proposals, maintenance records, pending-work requests, ongoing issues with any governmental agencies, open invoices and ongoing service contracts you should now have in your possession. The same goes for the basics such as the carpet type and manufacturer, exterior and interior paint color, appliance makes, models and sizes. Do you see the pattern here? We are trying to gather as much information about as much of our property as we can. This will help to minimize any surprises further on down the road. Surprises are exciting when it comes to love notes and birthday gifts only. There is no such thing as a good surprise for a landlord. There just isn't.

INVESTOR PROFILE

Name: Ron

Prior Occupation: Aerospace Engineer

Started Investing at Age: 39

First Investment: I bought a fourplex and I still own it today!

Current Real Estate Holdings: Over 200 units

Why Real Estate: Market values and rental rates increase over time, albeit slowly, thus increasing my financial return on investment.

I Wish I Knew When I Started That: I have no regrets over my own investments, but have had some frustrations with partnerships. The key to success in a partnership is knowing your partners and their interests. Aside from partnership hassles, it is important to understand the role that cheap debt plays on the artificial inflation of market values. Be wary of market values in times of cheap financing.

What I Look For in an Investment: Good financial return, can't be overpriced by the current market's standards.

To Those Starting Out, I Say: Read books and learn more about investing in real estate. I bought Nickerson's Book and I still own it today. It helped me make a lot of money! Join your apartment association and lastly if not most importantly…Don't sell! Buy real estate, fix it and hold it, but don't sell! Hold it long-term.

CHAPTER 13:
Build Your Budget

"We must consult our means rather than our wishes."

GEORGE WASHINGTON

Smart budgeting will help to prevent you from straying the path of success. In order for your budget to work as planned, it must be realistic, and it must be accurate. A complete and concise budget should include the full array of operating data from income collected to expenses paid. And while net income is key to the successful operation of your investment, it is positive cash flow that will essentially dictate just how successfully you are in operating it.

You see, without sufficient income to support the property, you will likely be paying your operating expenses and debt service out of your own pocket. Hopefully when you purchased your property, you put more forethought into your investment. That is, hopefully you purchased the property because it was going to make you money. Remember, there is a reason it is called an income property and not an outcome property: an income property should have money coming in and not coming out of your pocket.

So, how do we know what our net income was, is or should be? It's quite simple. First off, let's revisit one of the mathematic flows you likely considered when you first made your investment so that we understand the NOI figure. To arrive at the net income, we subtract the operating expenses from the gross income. Follow below:

Effective Gross Income
– Operating Expenses
= Net Operating Income (Net Income/NOI)
– Annual Debt Service
= Before Tax Cash Flow

Listed above are five lines that in their current form appear simple and harmless. Starting from the top line and working our way down, we will expand each category to include the details that will enable you to establish an effective projection of how the property will perform. Simply put, you want the number at the very top to be as high as possible and the number beneath it to be as realistic and minimal as possible.

In looking at these two numbers, we see where slumlords are born. You see, the slumlord will see the effective gross income and grow possessive and greedy. Uneasy and unwilling to part with this effective gross income, the slumlord does not maintain his property. Deferred maintenance builds up, and residents grow unhappy and move. The slumlord has shot himself in the foot, since he or she will ultimately lose income due to these vacancies and suffer lower market rents due to the lack of upkeep.

Always focus on income. Conduct your rental survey, and establish a realistic projection of the total income that you will receive. Be sure to factor in rental increases, vacancy rates, concessions, ancillary income, laundry income, pet rent, late fees, etc. This should be your projected gross income. Focus on the quality and the quantity of your income stream. Focus on preserving and maintaining this income stream. From here, we proceed downward to operating expenses.

Although I have placed heavy emphasis on the income portion of your budget, do not underestimate the importance of keeping your operating expenses down. Unfortunately, there are fewer potential sources of income than there are sources of operating expenses. You see, operating expenses are quite expansive and range from maintenance materials and labor to property taxes to marketing and utility expenses. Several factors will help you establish reasonable operating expenses when preparing your budget. These factors include the age of your property (new vs. old), the composition of your property (stucco vs. wood siding) and the climate in which your property is located. A newer property made of stucco and located in a warm, dry region will have less maintenance and fewer upkeep expenses than an older property made of wood siding and located in a cold, rainy region. Now, to prepare your budgeted expenses, look first to your current expenses.

Ask your broker for information (don't necessarily give the broker yours if they ask) and/or purchase from IREM (Institute of Real Estate Management) the operational data on multifamily properties such as yours. Be sure to compare the data accurately and understand how your property fits in with the comparable data. Are your expenses higher in some areas? Lower in some others? If so, why? What should you be doing to improve your operations? These are the questions you need to ask. Nothing will make you a better, more informed owner than understanding the simple nuances of your property. Know your property.

If you see glaring differences in your expenses, investigate the causes behind these expenses. Ask yourself, what is going wrong? Was the increase due to human error, mismanagement, not obtaining estimates or was there a huge expense that just threw things out of whack? Find out and prepare your budget. In California, maintenance expenses on a garden-style apartment property will run approximately 10% to 12% of EGI, with the total operating expenses at around 35% to 40% of EGI.

Start with the numbers you know to be true: the income, the property taxes and the debt service. Plug these numbers into your budget and proceed to estimate the approximate numbers of some of the other expenses. Be sure to plug in the market vacancy rate (I like to err on the high side). Now, start to plug in the other recurring expenses: utilities, pest control, pool guy, landscaper, utilities, you name it. Consult the sample sheet included herein.

Knowing all of this will allow you to obtain cost proposals from vendors ahead of time and agree on prices for the year with your chosen vendors. Sign a contract and then put it in your file. This will help to save you time during the year. The more detailed and precise you are with your estimating and budgeting, the less you have to fly by the seat of your pants during the year. And just think: when something comes up and needs to be done, you do not have to run around and get proposals; you already have them! That's what this is about. To be successful, you have to be prepared.

Review your budget on a monthly basis, and if you find that you do not meet it or you vary in certain areas, look into why. If you are consistently going over your budget, chances are that you need to reevaluate your expenses and project a more accurate budget. Remember, your budget is a living, breathing document. Be sure to monitor and follow it closely. If your numbers are off, re-forecast! There is nothing wrong with a mid-quarter, mid-year or other such re-forecast of your budget. It will be more accurate and result in less of a variance due to the actuality of the numbers, both income and expense.

CHAPTER 14:
The Ball is Rolling!

"It doesn't matter who scores the points. It's who gets the ball to the scorer that counts."

LARRY BIRD

With the setup work done, you are now ready to proceed in operating your business. Consider this the transition from a grand opening to the course of normal business duties. Although you have succeeded in establishing a good rapport with your customers, you now need to move on to the more important aspects of property ownership. This seemingly detailed and time consuming process can help keep you out of trouble and out of the courtroom. Additionally, it can help keep you and your property safe.

One thing that amazes me nowadays—not just in the property-management business, but with any business—is that some people still fail to make the correlation between happy customers and repeat business. If you are someone who genuinely cares, understand that this has a significant impact on your ROI. If you don't care now, you should! This is one of the non-monetary ways that you can increase the living experience for your residents. Master the art of caring or at least pretending to care. True, business is business. I am not expecting you to invite them over for dinner, but when you enter into their apartment, be kind and courteous. Don't be a jerk!

Remember, not all landlords are created equal. Like we discussed earlier, some landlords actually will show up in court with a McDonald's bag, napkin or paper towel. You may have bought his old property and it is now time to clean up the paperwork and maintenance issues left behind by such an amateur. A lot of this work can be done on your own, depending on your budget or time constraints. Any major concerns or red flags you come across in terms of lease paperwork or contracts should always be referred to your attorney. Otherwise, let's get on with improving your property.

Audit Your Leases & Paperwork

Landlord/tenant law is truly complex in nature. Additionally, and in conjunction with legislators, organizations such as Fair Housing work to police the rental industry from the bad guys, er, bad landlords. Laws, rules and regulations are constantly changing. It is imperative to stay up-to-date with your paperwork and utilize the newest and most accurate forms. You can get these from your apartment association or from the law firm with which you work.

These forms should include the necessary disclosures (i.e., lead-based paint, mold prevention, Prop 65, etc.). If you think it is expensive to purchase the forms, wait until you see the penalties and fines for violating Fair Housing laws. These fines can be excruciatingly devastating to property owners, often upwards of $10,000 per infraction. In some cases, and depending on circumstances, you can actually be forced to sell your property or pay for a management company to supervise the property while you are selling it.

The moral of the story is: be sure to follow the rules and keep your paperwork in order. Now that we have that out of the way, let's continue with lease audits. If you did this work during your due-diligence portion, you will not have to do it now.

Your current tenants might be locked into a fixed-term lease, or they might be in a month-to-month rental agreement. In either case, review the documents and establish what is missing, what is present and what is needed. If everything is there, then you are OK to proceed. If not, you will need to either wait until the lease expires, appropriately notify the residents of changes necessary and have them sign the new paperwork; or you can simply provide notice to the residents and require they sign the new forms if they are not locked into a contract.

If during the course of meeting your residents you found yourself meeting or coming across people who were obviously living at the property but were not on any sort of official documentation, you will want to have them apply to live at the property and satisfy all of your rental criteria. If they meet your criteria, then they should also complete the paperwork you require of your other residents.

Rental criteria? What rental criteria? You mean you actually have written guidelines on what it takes to rent from you? Of course!

Rental Criteria

> "What do I have to do to rent this place?"
> — Prospective Resident

That is one of the questions landlords love being asked the most. It's almost as good as "How would you like your steak cooked?" or "Here is my rent for the month of ..." In reality, the answer is quite simple: qualify. All your prospects have to do is meet and satisfy your rental criteria. Again, you will want to discuss your requirements with your attorney so that you can reinforce that you are not accidentally discriminating against someone.

Once the applicant completes his rental application and before you proceed with your background check, you will want to verify the identification and social security number put forth by the applicant on his application. With identity theft becoming more commonplace, it is important to make sure that your applicant is who he or she claims to be. Nowadays, there are a number of background check and screening programs that can identify the most minute of discrepancies, be it a previous address or transposed date of birth or something more significant like a fake social security number, eviction from a previous apartment complex or criminal record. Make sure that you leverage technology to your advantage.

So, what makes someone an ideal tenant? Well, they follow the rules and they pay rent on time. How can we determine whether or not someone will be a good tenant? There is no absolute guarantee, but there are a number of different items to consider. Paying rent on time requires someone to have income. Now, this can be from a number of legal, verifiable sources: jobs, subsidies, benefit programs and loans, but it is important to ensure that there will in fact be ample money in the tenant's bank account or wallet each month so that they can pay the rent. In qualifying the income, ask: How long have you been receiving this income and how long will you continue to receive it? In addition, request current documentation such as paystubs, grants, loan documents and other official information to support the income stated. Always, always, always call the source of income to verify that it is in fact legitimate, regardless of what documentation you receive. You want not only to verify that this is a current source of income, but also that it is likely to continue.

Part two of the verification should include a rental verification where you will clarify with previous landlords (at least one) that the applicant paid on time, gave proper notice, was not evicted, behaved appropriately and respected the property. You will likely find that the previously landlord will give you less but not more than you ask from him. It's OK. Take it and move on.

Part three of the verification process is the easiest and quickest part of the process. Having already done the verification of income and rental history, you will now conduct what is known as a comprehensive credit and background check. This should include: credit score from at least one of the three credit bureaus, nation- and state-wide criminal-background search, eviction check, bankruptcy detail and returned-check search. New searches are developing rapidly and include the capability of checking whether or not rent is paid on time at a current address if the landlord's management software is wired into the database. This is more or less icing on the cake and is unnecessary.

Once you have the rental and employment verifications, credit history and criminal and eviction checks completed, you can interpret the data and make your decision on whether or not to rent to this prospect. It is important to have pre-set, pre-determined criteria published in your marketing materials (website, flyers, blogs, Craigslist) so that applicants know what they need to do to rent the apartment. This will also help to refute any potential accusations of discrimination should an applicant be denied. It will not remove the possibility of these accusations entirely, and you cannot help being falsely accused, but you will certainly help yourself if you follow this process.

Now that we know what you should look for, let's look at the specifics.

Income is important since it is what enables the prospect to pay the rent. When establishing your qualifications, you will want to look at three key points:

How much is left over after expenses?

For how long has this income been received?

What are the prospects for it to continue?

You can consider income individually or collectively; however, you want to make sure that there will be enough money left over after the household expenses are paid for your prospective residents to pay rent. Consider it a comfort blanket of sorts, more or less a cushion that will help ensure that the rent will be received. The size of the buffer can vary by property type and or location. Typically, landlords ask for three times the monthly rent after expenses collectively and two times the monthly rent after expenses individually. Again, if you own property in an area where the tenant profile is less likely to meet the criteria because the rent is higher or perhaps residents do not make as much, you can consider adjustments.

Lastly, it is important to understand that income is income, so long as it is legal, documentable and verifiable. Refusing to rent to an applicant because you do not like where their money comes from is a form of discrimination. Remember to keep your opinions to yourself.

Rental history is equally important. Often times, resident managers or property owners will not comment on the status of an applicant's rental history, but they typically will verify whether or not the applicant has resided there and if they have given proper notice. That said, it is important to listen to what is not being said. What is the tone of the resident manager's voice as you are asking your questions? Are they happy to lose the residents and obviously relieved? Or are they disappointed to lose a good customer? Listen to what is not being said. Often times, it will tell you more than what is being said.

Give credit where credit is due. If your applicants have a proven track record of failing to fulfill their obligations, and their credit score reflects it, then most likely their rent will be no different. However, it is important to see what they are not paying. Late or unmade payments toward medical debt or student loans are not the same as repossessed vehicles or charged-off credit cards. Don't disqualify an applicant whose sole credit blemishes are the result of student loans or medical debt. These are increasingly common in this age of skyrocketing educational and medical costs, and not all people are fortunate enough to enjoy these luxury…necessities and must borrow to pay for them. This is different than borrowing and not honoring the promise to pay for the flat-screen television or the new SUV.

Seriously. One time at property, I noticed a 72-inch flat-screen television box by the dumpsters. I was impressed for a number of reasons: mostly because the television was more than double the size of my own television, but also because I was having a hard time imagining what a 72-inch television would look like on the walls of a 450-square-foot apartment. Who could have bought such a television? I found out soon enough. The buyer informed me that they could not pass up the opportunity to buy the television, and so they would have to pay their rent late. Proper screening can help you minimize this riff raff.

Another key step during the application-screening process is to conduct a criminal background check. Ensuring your safety as well as that of your customers is of the utmost importance. Be sure to ask appropriate questions on your rental application and verify the criminal records of your applicants. Any lies on the application should result in immediate disqualification. Additionally, you should ask your landlord/tenant attorney about the rules in your area for not renting to convicted criminals who have committed violent or drug offenses. Rules vary widely by city and state, so be sure to verify for yourself before you advertise your requirements in your rental criteria.

Now that you have established your rental criteria, you can proceed to market and lease your vacant apartment homes. Once occupancy is restored and you are full or at a tolerable occupancy level for your market, you can turn your focus to the upkeep and preservation of your property. Not only will this serve as preventative maintenance, it will also help in attracting residents you actually want. Think about it: Do you care about where you live? Would you let the stucco become discolored and crack at your own home? How would you feel if the grass was dead and the landscape was drab? Better yet, how would you feel if the fascia boards were peeling so badly it looked like you were going to be attacked by splinters every time you walked by?

Allow me to answer for you. You would not appreciate it and you would hate coming home. Apartments are no different. If you want to be a slumlord, I cannot help you. Well, actually I can. That is, the court system, the City or the Housing Authority can appoint me or a professional like me to manage your property if you do not take care of it. You see, the whole point is to attract quality residents who care about where they live. In order to do so, you have to provide a quality place to live. This has nothing to do with the location of the property and everything to do with the upkeep of the property. People who care about where they live pay on time and refer their friends and family who also pay on time. There is a direct correlation between the upkeep of your property and the quality of the income stream associated with it. The sooner you realize this, the better.

Curb Appeal

You have been spending a lot of time at your property and have realized that it needs a few things. So, you pick up your vendor list and schedule to meet with contractors to obtain cost estimates on some repairs. While there are certain items that can always do wonders for a property: new exterior paint, landscape and new signage, there are a lot of items that can become necessary although they will not necessarily bring you any more money.

Begin your audit from the curb inward. I like to refer to this as the "curb to carports" or "gutters to garages" inspection in that you are starting at the very front of your property and working your way to the rear of the property, painstakingly noting any deferred maintenance, improvements or other items that you would like to revisit along the way. So, why start out front? Well, imagine that you are a prospective resident and you see the ad on the Internet. You print the directions and drive to the property. Once there, you get out of the car and step forward. This very instant, you can be sold. However, the property must meet or exceed your requirements.

Now, every resident or prospective resident will have different concerns. And it is important that they have concerns because if they do not care about where they live, why will they take care of their apartment home? They won't. They will destroy it, and you will spend a small fortune cleaning the apartment home up and making it ready for the next resident. So, start with a very simple assessment and just look for the following items. Remember, when it comes to where you live, looks are deceiving—very deceiving in some cases. So make sure that the very least your property has the following items under control.

Curb Appeal Checklist 101

- Is the grass green and grown in or are there a number of dry, dead spots?
- Are there seasonal, colored flowers planted across the property?
- Is the concrete well-paved or is it bumpy and full of holes?
- Is the stucco clean, crisp and colorful or is it discolored and faded?
- Are the gutters clean or are there sticks and leaves spilling out?
- Is the fascia or header board painted and sealed nicely or is it cracked and chipping?
- Is the front door on the office or the vacant unit freshly painted?

Just as you compile your list of upgrades that you must make to the apartment complex, the prospective resident is essentially quantifying whether or not the complex meets their standards. Chances are, the prospect's list of reasons and your list of improvements or non-improvements will have similarities. If you have considered introducing any of the aforementioned improvements, it is always recommendable to do so. Remember: You ain't foolin' no one. If you notice that the stucco is busted and the grass is dead, you know that it's because you have another full-time job, or you have been out of town. The prospective resident just thinks you are a money-grubbing slumlord. Don't be that guy (or gal)!

Work diligently to ensure that your property looks its best at all times. This means: free of trash, green lawns, colored flowers, fresh looking stucco and trim. Sell the prospect on your property before they even see the interior. It is very possible.

Maintenance

Preventative maintenance for an apartment owner is like a laser-aim for a sharp shooter: not entirely necessary, but very important and very helpful. Keeping up on preventative maintenance will save you money over the long haul since you can prevent the big mishaps by spending for small fixes along the way. Unfortunately, it is not always about the small fixes. Sometimes, you will have big-ticket items come up and it is important to be able to respond intelligently. For this reason, it is a good idea to troubleshoot ahead of time. Yes, this makes you pro-active as opposed to reactive, and this is what property management is all about.

So, reach out to your vendors. Let them know that you have something planned for later in the year or perhaps next year, but you wanted to get some solid budget numbers in place so that you can proceed with the work once the cost is feasible. Then, have your vendors provide estimates on these big-ticket items. Remember to get three proposals. Now, the big-ticket items will be property specific, but generally speaking these items can or will include:

- new roof
- new central water heater
- upgrade to copper plumbing if applicable
- new gated entry system
- new central heat/air system if applicable

Your property may have more items that you should consider, but you can discover those as you get to know your property. Be sure to pay attention to the routine maintenance repairs and requests that you receive from your tenants. If you are constantly replacing or repairing the same things, you might want to look into them a little closer and see what you might be able to do to prevent them from malfunctioning so often.

Nothing will disappoint or irritate your residents more than ignoring or avoiding their maintenance requests. Do not be the landlord who dismisses his tenant's requests. With the various internet review sites today, you can become public enemy number one in no time. When people see your ads online and want to learn more about your property, they will Google your address and read the negative reviews. Unfortunately, they will not always call you to clarify. This goes back to our approach to customer service: remember to be pro-active and not reactive.

Regarding the specific telephone number at which residents should contact you, be advised that you should shut this phone off after hours or when you are not looking to be bothered. It is perfectly fine to record a message that states what a resident should do in a specific circumstance. For example, your recording should sound something like:

"Thank you for calling the Such-and-Such Apartments. Your call is important to us. Please leave a message and we will return your call during our next business hours. If you are a resident calling with an after-hours plumbing emergency, please call (give the phone number). Realize if this is not an emergency, you will be charged. If this is an absolute emergency due to fire, flood or blood, please be sure to call 911. Thank you."

That's it. That's all. You're done. You are happy, and they are happy.

Rental Survey

Yes, that rental survey. So, if you were smart and followed directions during the due-diligence process, you will have all the information on hand that you will ever need. If you did not, well, that's fine too. You just didn't follow directions and will have to start from scratch. Since this is the WPMS portion of the book, that is what we will do.

So, now that your paperwork (leases, applications and other operating documents) is in order and your physical upkeep is solid, you should begin what will soon become one of the most important documents in your managerial operation: the **rental survey**. A rental survey is a complete and concise document that effectively details the availability, product type, rent rate, concessions, unit mix, square footage and amenities of all comparable properties. In preparing your rental survey, you will want to account for all relevant properties in your area. This could be as few as four, it could be as many as 15. When it comes to data, more is always better.

If you are unsure of where to start, you can always contact the broker from whom you purchased the property and have them send you their rental survey from when they facilitated the transaction. Otherwise, you will want to begin visiting the properties and accounting for the necessary data. You will want to tell the on-site personnel of the properties you visit that you own property in the area and that you are conducting a rental survey. It is always nice if you offer to share the survey as well. This will also help you to evaluate the management company who takes over management of your properties should you hire one. Are you paying the company to keep rents low so that their job is easier? No, you're not. So, know your market and know your competition. It will be to your benefit to see firsthand who is in the marketplace and who could potentially be of assistance should your current management company not work out.

Now, I recommend touring the properties in person the first time around. Not only will this help you to establish a visual connection and understanding with the competing properties, it will help establish a bond so that you can communicate effectively by phone in the future. It will eventually become as easy as a telephone call stating, "Hi, it's Nicholas with So-and-So Apartments. Any updates on your rental survey?" Remember to take notes and take away any pamphlets or brochures. Always, always, always ask about specials and move-in incentives. A lot of times, a property will market one rate in print or online, but will feature a teaser rate at the property level. This is the actual rent with which you are competing.

You can use as much or as little data as you like, but remember that what you are trying to arrive at is the effective price point for your apartment home in the specific rental submarket in which it is located. Obviously you are not going to directly compare a garden-style 1960s complex to a brand-new loft space in AAA location, but you will want to know what that loft is renting for so that you can determine your price and market it accordingly. Just like with any business, knowing your product and where it fits in the local marketplace will help you set prices and appeal to customers. Once you arrive at what you feel is an appropriate market rent for your vacant apartment homes, you are ready to put them on the market.

INVESTOR PROFILE

Name: Paul

Prior Occupation: Merchant Marine

Started Investing at Age: 24

First Investment: I Partnered in a 6 unit complex with 2 friends. We were able to each put together $15k and purchase the property on a land contract.

Current Real Estate Holdings: Partner in over 800 apartment units, 2 office buildings and student housing

Why Real Estate: The four benefits! This is a business where you can build equity and cash flow as well as control the management and operation of your investment. You do not have this option with other passive investments.

I Wish I Knew When I Started That: The art of delegating tasks and projects and the importance of taking care of your investments. Hands-on operation of your real estate investments is the key to success.

What I Look For in an Investment: Positive cash flow and upside potential through the value-add process.

To Those Starting Out, I Say: Clearly identify your goals and objectives for investing. So often, people are unclear and end up disappointed. You need to have specific requirements. Just saying, "I want to make money", will not make you successful. You need to clearly define, quantify and enumerate your goals for your desired financial returns. During your working years you want to position yourself for growth so that in your non-working years you are positioned for cash flow.

NICHOLAS A. DUNLAP

CHAPTER 15:
Marketing in Motion

"The head of PR is perhaps one of the most important people in a company, and a good Chairman will have them by their side. They are critical in managing the brand and can save millions in advertising; (what) people are saying bout your Company is much more important than any advertising."

SIR RICHARD BRANSON

Yes. This is the world we live in. While we can spend thousands or more on our marketing budget, nothing works better than good old public relations. See, we can play the role of "good guy" whom people simply like, and as a result, to whom they would like to refer their friends and family. And while this is certainly a best practice for our business, it is often overlooked. Keep this in mind as you start marketing your apartment homes to the public.

You've done all of your homework and you are now ready to advertise your vacant apartment homes for rent. But where do you start? Really, where should you start? There are thousands of effective marketing outlets nationwide, and some sources are free advertising and some are paid. In any case, you will want to maximize your exposure and be visible anywhere and everywhere you can. A complete marketing plan will include flyers to residents, a poster in the laundry room and a Craigslist advertisement. Depending on the area in which your property is located, you might find that one source of advertising is more effective than another. The sooner you find that out, the better.

So, start with research. Where are your competitors advertising? If they are in the town paper and that is what fills their vacancies, guess what: you need to be there, too!

Flyers

One of the best ways to attract new residents is to advertise to them through your current customers. Having established a good rapport with your residents, you are likely known as the "cool new landlord who bought them pizza" or the "new owner who put in the new land-scaping and cleaned up the property." With such glowing recommen-dations, it is an absolute must for you to solicit their help in renting your units. You can do this a number of ways, including:

Offering a rent discount to your current residents if their referral signs a year lease. Always do this after the referral has been there at least one month so you avoid any potential problems, like losing your money.

Offer a gift card to your current residents if their referral is approved and signs a one-year lease.

Again, these are cool things that you can do for a minimal expense. More importantly, they start at the property level and will help you harness the power of resident referrals. Often times, these are your best residents who are in turn referring their friends or family who will also become good residents. We're not talking rocket science, here. The flyers should be simple and to the point. Sometimes the most effective flyers read:

Now Renting! 2 Bedroom/2 Bath with Upgrades!
Refer a friend and get $250 dollars off of your Rent! Call for details!
— *Management*

Distribute these in person or by mail to your residents ahead of a vacancy. You will get calls. In fact, something is wrong if you do not get calls. Earlier on, we discussed the importance of maintaining favorable relations with your residents. This is where the referral flyer comes in handy. As you visit the property, keep a couple cards in your back pocket and pass them on to your current residents.

Poster

It's not like it sounds. Not the tacky fluorescent paper signs plastered up on telephone poles by concert promoters. No. By poster I mean a flyer, say legal size paper more or less. However, this poster should be situated in a relevant common area or two. This could be the mailbox area, certainly the laundry room, perhaps the swimming-pool area, etc. At minimum, you should include a color copy of the Craigslist advertisement. At most, you can customize a flyer to include the specifics. Remember, if you are going to spend a lot of money on any sort of advertising, I highly recommend leaving the price off of it. Unfortunately, if the public does not take to your price and you are forced to reduce the rent, you will also be forced to trash your marketing materials. That is, unless you don't include the price. Plus, more people will call you out of interest if you do not include the price. And what you want is to rely on your sales skills to close the deal. Remember: the people aspect is always the wild card.

Yes, when it comes to price information, you want to include less, not more. Including too much or all of the information can prevent people from calling you. If you leave out information, they have to call you to find out about the price, about the pet policy or about the parking situation. Your conversation with the prospective resident will tell you a lot and will help you understand whether you have selected an effective price point for your apartment homes.

While you want to test the market and attempt to achieve top market rents, you also want to minimize the downtime, rent loss and other headaches and difficulties associated with the vacant apartment. To minimize your loss to vacancy, you need to maximize your advertising efforts. Not necessarily your budget, but at the very least your efforts!

Craigslist

For apartment owners, Craigslist is the best thing since sliced bread. Ultra effective, free advertising that allows owners to reach a more qualified, sophisticated consumer. Price shopping, amenity shopping and location shopping is all done online. That said, once the prospective resident arrives at the community, they have done their homework and are further along in their decision process. Statistics show that most consumers begin their search online.

So what makes a Craigslist ad effective? There are several things to consider when placing your ads, but more important are the circumstances of when and what. Craigslist tends to be more effective for apartment owners either early in the morning or later in the evening. Sure, there are browsers throughout the day, but most people either get to work and look for their new place and decide who they will call on their lunch break or they look once they get home for who they will call the following day.

Whether you use a nicely designed template from Postlets (http://www.postlets.com) , a service that will also syndicate your rental listing out to dozens of free listing sites, or you do it yourself and include a few photos and brief textual explanation, as long as you use good pictures and include a phone number, you should do fine. If you put up an ad and do not get calls, check to see that your ad is still up. If your ad is up and you are not getting calls, then it might be time for a new ad.

Now, you might find in your market that your Postlets template is not effective and maybe a traditional Craigslist ad with just a few photographs of the property and some basic detail does the trick. Whatever the case may be, track the response that you receive to each of your ads. This will help you gauge and understand what the most effective form of advertising is for your property.

Facebook

Facebook is fast becoming the worlds preferred method of communication. If you did not know that, you need help. While you might personally boycott Facebook for your own silly reasons, it is important to embrace Facebook for business. For those of you who live underneath a rock, social media continues to change the way that business is done. And unlike other forms of social media, Facebook allows you to showcase and include specific information such as phone numbers, addresses, business hours and photos. Just think: You can establish a Facebook business page for your property for free and use the account to communicate with prospective and or current residents.

Using Facebook as a tenant portal is not only a resident-retention tool, but also an excellent piece of free marketing. Establish your presence on the web and maintain it for free. Remember how we talked about the flyers that you will give to your residents, or the posters that you will put up on-site? Well, this is the online version. Now, there is so much cool stuff that you can do with your social media marketing. You can easily link from your Craigslist ad to your Facebook page for additional information. Thus, by the time your prospects contact you, they have seen two different sets of photos of your property and have read the specifics as well.

In creating and maintaining a Facebook page for your property, you will also help to control some of what comes up in a Google search when your property's street address is keyed in. Just like you want to have full control of your property in person, you will also want to maintain control online. Say your property is named "Wilshire Villas." If you Google "Wilshire Villas" and the first five pages or links relate to a roach problem, rodent issues, drug use or other unsavory content, you are in trouble. In that case, you not only have work to do on-site but you may even want to look into a specialty company that can help you restrict the content that registers in a search of your property name or address. Think about it: If you are going to spend money on your on-line advertising, you should make sure that you are not wasting your money.

In Print

Paid advertising is also a valid source to consider, but it is important to monitor this expense closely and also to refrain from signing any long-term contracts. Depending on the property, magazines such as *For Rent*, *Apartment Guide* or *Apartment Magazine* are somewhat struggling to keep up with Craigslist and other online advertising venues. As such, their rates have somewhat decreased in recent years. If you get a good deal, you may want to consider it.

Local papers or journals like the Pennysaver can also be effective. However, this is another advertising method that either works or doesn't work based on a specific geographical region, submarket or demographic.

Often times, these magazines turn into the Sears catalogs from years past. That is, they get picked up, read through and highlighted, but the items never make it home. They are the window-shoppers' special. At least with Craigslist you have to manually input your search criteria. One of the key statistics to track is the "cost to lease" as it relates to your advertising budget. How much are you spending to lease your apartment homes? If the Pennysaver or one of the regional newspapers costs $650 per lease, where *Apartment Guide* is only $300, then *Apartment Guide* is obviously the better choice. Facebook and Craigslist are free, so they have an even better cost per lease. That's $0 for you reading along at home that might not be the best at math.

On-Site

We have already discussed the flyers to current residents and the posters in the common areas; however, we need to now discuss how we are going to dress the property up for your prospective resident. Gimmicks, banners, signs, balloons, big boys, you name it. Your options are limitless. Generally speaking, the more festive the setup is, the more positive. Balloons work great and keep things festive. You can tie them to mailboxes, the handrails, trees, signage, the roof, etc.

The actual vacant unit should be staged and should include a Glade air freshener, nice shower curtain and bath mat, doormat in the entryway, potted plants, candles, etc. There are a number of inexpensive things that can be done to dress up the apartment home so as to create a memorable experience to all prospective residents who tour the property. Remember, you want people to think of this as home. So … make it home! While it is important to diversify your advertising to include online, print and word-of-mouth campaigns, it is even more important to watch your property closely and see what works for you. Your initial focus should be on brining in the prospective residents, but once the prospective residents get to the property, you must be sure to impress them so that you can hopefully keep them and one day have them as residents. Remember that in order to maximize your rents you have to maximize your marketing. If you expect to get top market rent with no advertising, you are going to suffer through extended periods of vacancies. So, get creative and get after it.

You want your prospective residents to fall in love with your property and envision themselves living in your apartment homes. Once the prospect establishes a personal connection with the apartment, it is easy to get them to apply. But it's all about the personal connection and reaching the customer. You will not reach everyone—at least, you shouldn't. But hey, 90% isn't bad.

Is It Time For a Special?

As you've gathered by now, I will not tell you how to run your business, but I will tell you what you can do better. So, if after following each of these steps you are still not receiving calls or applications on your vacant apartment home, you should look at your market rents. Although it depends on individual preference, I would rather adjust rents after two-and-a-half weeks of intensive marketing than allow the apartment home to continue to sit vacant. Sometimes the market is tough and we are forced to introduce concessions to attract renters. That said, there is a difference between undercutting the landlord next door and adjusting your prices to meet the market. Do not let your pride get in the way of allowing you to adjust your rents. Make the adjustment, rent the apartment home and get on with your life.

In response to the market or in an effort to meet it, you can try two things. The first and otherwise easiest thing to do is just to reduce rent. Call back your prospects, refresh the ad on Craigslist and gauge your response. Or, if the situation is drastic and calls for drastic measures, then introduce some sort of move-in special. A move-in special can include a number of things, but generally involves a decreased security deposit, discounted rent or other such promotional item to generate interest. Now, just like you set your rental criteria, you need to ensure that you set specific criteria for your move-in specials. While you are at it, be sure to include the acronym "OAC" in your advertising. This is short for "on approved credit." This way, you do not get someone who would not qualify under any circumstances looking for the special. Unfortunately, this happens with specials. People are attracted by the artificially low rates or low move-in costs. Of course, this is the intent. However, you want to ensure that you are attracting prospects who qualify based on your standards or rental criteria. Think OAC and protect yourself.

NICHOLAS A. DUNLAP

CHAPTER 16

Grease the Wheels

"The course of true love never did run smooth."

WILLIAM SHAKESPEARE

The first few months of property ownership are almost like the honeymoon phase of a new marriage or relationship. Things are great and just seem too easy—so easy, in fact, that you suddenly find yourself contemplating a new purchase. Right about then, the inevitable happens. Your residents have outgrown the honeymoon phase and have started to complain. And that's OK. You see, it's all about balance. You must juggle your highs and lows and put in place the policies and procedures that will not just make you successful, but allow you to sleep comfortably at night.

So, a tenant complains. Let's say they complain about maintenance that needs to be done. And it may even be something that they broke. Now, it is important to remember two things as you approach the situation. While this is your investment, your nest egg, your retirement, your cash flow, whatever financial purpose it serves to you, it is their home. Someone comes here after a long day at work and helps their children do homework. Someone becomes disappointed, upset or depressed and wants comfort, and they come here. For you, it is work, for them it is home. You certainly appreciate their patronage; now, respect their human needs.

One of the frustrating, er, enjoyable aspects of property management is the human interaction or interface that you get to have with your customers. Now, let's not kid ourselves. There will be times you have to deal with people in less-than-favorable circumstances. Know that. Just like you own this property as an investment, they lack the financial wherewithal to own property and, as a result, expect to be taken care of in the space that they rent. So, while some residents will be what Michael Stipe of the Rock Group R.E.M. would refer to as "Shiny, Happy People," others will be negative vampires out to suck your blood. Do not allow this to happen.

The Threatening Resident

Smart property owners are efficient with their efforts and effective with their communication. You see, part of what you need to know and what you need to illustrate to your residents is that just because they say they need or want something does not make it right. For example: carpet/flooring needs to be replaced, dishwasher needs to be replaced, they need a new air-conditioning unit, toilet seat or light bulb. Needs and wants are often disguised as ransom-like threats to property owners.

> "If I don't get my new AC, then I'm moving."
> — *Angry Tenant*

Sometimes it's that easy, and residents will simply threaten us with their request and provide us with an ultimatum. Luckily for us, when residents are that forthcoming about things, it enables us to decide easily whether or not we will consider the repairs. In adherence to your budget, you can decide for or against these repairs. It is important to realize that the more you give in to these requests, the more likely you are to receive them. One week it's the new AC unit, and the next its new carpet for his neighbor. Before you know it, there is a $1,500 variance to your budget.

By this time, you may be perfectly fine with the resident moving on. If that's the case, so be it. I am not a proponent of trying to make everyone happy. I am a proponent of doing what makes you happy while doing what is right for others and right for your property. Often times this is a win-win, but this can be a slippery slope. Do not allow yourself to be bamboozled by your residents. Your residents are smart people who will spot sensitivity and try to capitalize on it. Don't be a reactive fool; be a pro-active property owner.

Prepping Your Vendors

The squeaky wheels get the grease, or at least that's the saying. Be sure to take care of and appease your residents, but do not allow yourself to be forced into anything or put into a situation or position where your residents are given the proverbial "upper hand." To minimize liability or to ensure that you are taking the necessary steps when solving a problem, you should send in an outside contractor to survey the scene. Advise the contractor ahead of time to keep his or her mouth shut while inside of the apartment home and to discuss their findings solely with you once the detail is finished.

You'd be amazed how often a vendor will go into an apartment to do work, completely disregard that he or she is being paid by the property owner and proceed to speak openly, bad-mouth or otherwise comment to the tenant while exaggerating the nature of the problem. The first time you hear of something like this happening, remove the vendor from your list and add another one in their place. Do not give bad vendors second chances. There are too many good vendors out there for you to be attached to one. When this does not happen, know that you have a good vendor in your stable, and continue to use them.

The After-Hours Emergency

Another situation you will encounter is the late-night emergency. This could be a slab leak, lock out or other such issue. As we discussed early on, you will want to have pre-recorded information available to your residents so that the problem can be resolved effectively without requiring your immediate attention. There are no laws requiring you to respond after-hours in California, but you will likely want to consult your local apartment association or your attorney to make sure that there are not any local requirements of which you are unaware. A properly drafted lease agreement will protect you from headaches and nonsense like this, but if it can wait until business hours (chances are that it can) then let it wait.

Scenario: So, it's 2:00am on Saturday night and your resident notices their kitchen floor getting warm. He does not think anything of it, and he goes to bed. He wakes up in the morning, and his apartment is flooded. He calls you, but you do not answer. He hears your voice message greeting, which provides him with the preferred-plumbers information that he should use with an emergency such as this one. He calls the plumber, and you are not bothered. Monday morning, you turn on your "management" cell phone and learn of the incident. You follow up with the resident, offer to take care of him, perhaps buy him a gift card to a local restaurant, check to see that the work was completed correctly and that the apartment is in satisfactory condition. And you're done! What could you have done at 2:00am? Wake up, get online and look for a plumber who would overcharge you anyway? No. Don't set yourself up for that. Exercise forethought and pro-activity, not reactivity.

Follow these steps, and you will live to acquire another multifamily property. Or, you might decide that you want to own office or industrial buildings instead. Don't become so miserable that you will go on to make rash decisions like selling at the wrong time and missing out on some of the prime benefits of owning real estate such as equity buildup, tax shelter and cash flow. This is what we are trying to avoid. Remember, you've got plenty of options!

You can always consider hiring a management company to look after your properties, but being as you are reading this portion on self-management, it is obviously not your first choice. If given the choice between selling and hiring a management company, I highly recommend hiring a management company. You know the vendor selection process already: interview three companies and then choose one. It is important for you to understand how property management works so that if you choose to hire a company to manage on your behalf, you know the basics of what they are doing. You know whether you are getting your money's worth or should be getting more for your money.

INVESTOR PROFILE

Name: Jerome

Prior Occupation: Student

Started Investing at Age: 23

First Investment: A rundown Single Family Residence

Current Real Estate Holdings: 30,000 units nationwide – valued in excess of $2.5 billion dollars

Why Real Estate: The finance professors in grad school for business preached that the markets were efficient and one could not outperform an index fund. The real estate professors said you could make money "buying low and selling high". Real estate is the largest asset class and very inefficient market allowing an entrepreneur a chance to make money. Real estate also allows high-low cost leverage enabling the sponsor of a partnership or syndication to make big leverage bets.

I Wish I Knew When I Started That: Business school doesn't teach you the practical aspects of acquiring, owning and operating real estate or how to add value to a property.

What I Look For in an Investment: At least a 15% leveraged IRR over a 5 year holding period to allow for an investor to double their money. 20% IRR is preferred. High single to double-digit cash on cash returns are also preferred. I like to buy at significant discounts in high barrier to entry markets.

To Those Starting Out, I Say: Get as much education as you can early in life. Work for a firm that is entrepreneurial or learn from someone who pursues value add or opportunistic acquisitions. Outwork your peers and network intensely within your industry.

Hiring Your Team

"Do not hire a man (or woman) who does your work for money, but him (or her) who does it for the love of it."

HENRY DAVID THOREAU

With the right personnel in place, your job as property owner can become almost simple. However, hiring the right people for the job is a job in itself. Do not underestimate the act of hiring the right person for the job. And just as one hire can simplify your life and relieve you off added or unwanted stress, making the wrong hire can turn your dreams into nightmares. But wait, it gets better. (That was sarcasm.) As both a housing provider and an employer, you share double the liability of most employers. What's more, you are entrusting someone with access to all the worldly belongings of your tenants. Make the wrong hire, and you could end up in a nasty lawsuit over pleasant things like: theft, burglary, negligence or assault. Take your hiring job seriously.

Most states require an apartment building with 16 or more units to have a "responsible person" on-site. No, your residents are not con- sidered responsible. This law refers to someone that you as the owner have a written agreement with to represent, or at the very least look after or represent, your interests on-site. This can be a **resident manager** or a **maintenance tech**. This can be someone referred to as a key-keeper or even a handyman. The duties you choose to assign to this person will be at your discretion. You can choose to employ them to the extent you'd like to employ them. If you want them just to keep an eye out, then make sure you get your agreement in writing and make sure that you are clear on how this person will be compensated. Remember, we are trying to keep you out of the court-room. Back to staffing: Hiring the right person, be it a managerial or maintenance employee, will make your life so much easier. So, let's get started.

A good resident manager is like a running back's right knee. That is, when it's healthy the team wins, but when it buckles the team fails. As such, a resident manager should possess strong sales and marketing skills, time-management skills (extremely important), people skills for customer service, problem-solving skills and a positive attitude. Saying things the right way is a gift. Some people have it, and some do not. Do not hire someone who does not have it. One good test to use when hiring a resident manager is to ask him or her to show you a vacant apartment home as though you were a prospective resident. Allow them the opportunity to demonstrate their skills in action, not just through the interview process. You might be surprised. Sometimes, the people with the right answers are not the most effective on-the-job.

After you interview your prospective employee, be sure to provide them with an application where you can obtain all of their verifi-able information. Once you verify their identity, proceed with their background and credit check. These are equally important to the hiring process. For one, you want to make sure that you are not hiring someone with poor credit to the extent that they could possibly want to steal money from you or your property (they manage your prop-erty and will have access to it). Next, you want to make sure that they do not have a criminal record of any kind. Here again, it is important to consult your local apartment association or other business group such as the Chamber of Commerce to ensure that you are in compli-ance with local requirements for employers. Now, aside from that, can you imagine explaining that one in court or in a deposition? I think it would play out like this:

> "Your honor, I did know she had previous drug offenses and an assault charge, but I didn't think she would steal from me. And yes, I did give her the keys to my residents' apartments."
> — *Stupid Property Owner*

This is not going to be you. Seriously, this is not going to be you. You screen your residents, so be sure that you screen your employees as well. Wouldn't you want to know who was going in and out of your home? Would you want this person going in and out of your own home? I didn't think so.

A lot of people will make the mistake of requiring their resident manager to complete maintenance and repairs. This is not only wrong in the sense that your managers are not skilled maintenance workers, but it is also wrong in that you are drawing them away from what they should be doing. A successful owner will use their managers for one thing and one thing only: to manage. Be sure you have a concise job description and employment contract for your prospective manager to sign once they have been hired. Accurately describe the tasks they will complete on a daily basis and the total compensation they will receive in accordance with the hours they log.

Realize that there are limits on the amount of time someone works that you can credit towards a rent-free apartment. Meaning that in exchange for an apartment and without monetary compensation, you can only use a certain amount of the rent to satisfy minimum-wage requirements. In laments terms, this means that you cannot require your resident managers to work more than a certain amount of hours per week unless you are actually paying them a salary. The rent credit or rent-free apartment in exchange for resident-manager duties is great for smaller properties, but on bigger properties that require more work from an employee, you will need to figure out a salary that allows you to meet the minimum-wage requirements.

Remember, just because they live on-site does not mean that they are always working. A resident manager must only work during their allotted, posted office hours. Look, this is a sensitive issue. And since my experience is with mostly California and Texas, I speak based on this experience. Make sure that you obtain from your attorney or from your apartment association an employee agreement that will protect you.

Unfortunately, you will also need to realize that we live in the 21st Century, and it is imperative for you to follow the rules so as to not become the victim of an opportunistic leach, looking to make a quick buck by playing and winning the "lawsuit lottery." Be sure to consult the appropriate source for legal information with regard to the aforementioned details and arrange a scenario that will specifically fit your property size and pay scale.

Having hired the right person, you will now need to establish the daily, weekly and monthly tasks that your resident manager will complete for you. On a monthly basis, the resident manager should collect rents, post notices, conduct a rental survey and provide you with a summary of activity at the property (who moved in, who gave notice and who moved out). On a weekly basis, the resident manager should account for maintenance requests, traffic logs or summary of calls from advertisements, a summary of activity similar to the monthly reports. On a daily basis, the manager should clean up the property, look for any items requiring maintenance (graffiti, stucco damage, broken glass) and notify the appropriate vendor, market and lease vacant apartment homes, interface with residents and keep the place in shape. It is an easy job that gets even easier when the property is 100% occupied. At this point, an efficient resident manager can clean up the property and field requests from the comfort of their living-room couch with their favorite daytime soaps or talk shows sounding in the background. You may require less, different or additional information than that, but at the very least, you need to have the weekly calls, maintenance and operational activity logged in your records. These reports are the best way to ensure accuracy in your record keeping and also to monitor property activity. As a side note, these reports can also help to ensure that you are keeping your on-site people honest.

Later on, we will explore how you can hire a professional management company to insulate you from some of the headaches of property operation and more importantly, to help to streamline the investment process.

NICHOLAS A. DUNLAP

CHAPTER 18:
Protecting Your Reputation

"It takes 20 years to build a reputation and five minutes to ruin it. If you think about that, you'll do things differently."

WARREN BUFFET

Whether you manage your property yourself, hire a resident manager to take care of the on-site duties or hire a management company to manage for you, it is important to realize that you will always be the subject of ignorant, uninformed and opinionated commentary on your ownership and management methods. As philistine or obnoxious as these opinions might be, realize that they often spawn from specific circumstances or situations. Take the time to look into and understand where these comments are coming from. If you start to notice a commonality or similarity, delve deeper. Have you done something wrong? Could you stand to handle yourself differently in the presence of your customers? Sometimes, people overreact or maybe even respond in kind to the foolishness with which they are faced. Reserve your reactions for the ride home; also read, "Keep your cool."

All it takes is one unfavorable interaction with a customer, either current or prospective to start a smear campaign. And unfortunately, the technology available today makes it easier for people to criticize and comment on occurrences at your property. Websites like Yelp, Apartment Ratings and Apartment Reviews offer forums for the public to log on and type in your property's address and name and anonymously talk trash on you and your property. Even worse, Google actually associates this data with your property name and address so that if you Google your property address, this information will pop up. Now, if something offensive or obscene is written, the website will typically remove it. But the fairly common exaggerations and/or lies that people often use in these reviews will not. Therefore, you need to approach the situation from another angle.

Your angle is cool, calm and even-tempered. You do not address these issues; you simply respond and express your concern. For example, a tenant moves out and writes: "This place is a dump. I had rats in my apartment and the manager smoked pot all day. Don't live here." OK, now any level-headed person is going to read this review and think that the reviewer is nuts. So, what you are going to do is this. First, take advantage of the "I'm the manager" or "I'm the owner" capability that these websites offer—some charge, and some provide the capability for free. Then, pay the nominal fee and take the necessary steps to protect your reputation. Now, if there is truth to any of the complaints, you will have some work to do on-site. In the meantime, let's get to clearing up our online reputation.

A couple of chapters back, we discussed the importance of good PR versus good advertising and how controlling your Google search results will help you in the operation of your multifamily property. Well, here we are taking one more step to protect your interests. You see, it is not just about your response, it is about publically fostering good relations with your residents, your customers and your potential customers. It is not just a generic, canned response. It is a chance to connect. Do not miss your chance. So, you notice the negative review that has just appeared on the review website du jour. Log on and respond to the agitated, unsavory or unhappy and inflammatory post as follows:

> "I'm sorry your stay at XYZ apartments was less than
> satisfactory. Realize that it is our goal to provide a quality
> living experience to all of our residents. Since we provide

a full-service maintenance staff and have a pest-control vendor on retainer, we certainly would have addressed your concerns had you brought them to us. Hopefully, you will give us a chance to demonstrate our exceptional service to you sometime in the future."

Thank you,
XYZ Apartments

This is simple, to the point and avoids arguing with someone who might be an imbecile but who also might have some valid concerns. Once again, you want to exhibit concern, but also diminish their credibility by stating the facts if they exist. Do this in a robotic manner each and every time you receive one of these reviews. Now, I mean robotic in the sense of responding quickly and effectively, not in that the response is robotic. (If your response is robotic, your customers will pick up on this, and it will not win them over. Look what it did for Mitt Romney.) Now, remember the old saying: "Don't argue with fools, for people from a distance can't tell who is who." By simply responding and not engaging, you are taking the appropriate step in bypassing future conflict. You are taking the wind out of their sail. You see, these people are obviously not concerned about anything. If they were, they would have brought the issue to your attention or to your resident manager, for that matter.

Just as Google links your property's name and address to these reviews, Google can also be a resource to you with regard to your online reputation. Log on to Google and type in Google Alerts. A Google alert will email you anytime that someone types in specific information or content about you or your property on the Internet. Setup a Google alert with your property name and address. Respond to each and every bit of feedback you receive. This will help you personally as well. Every property owner needs a Google alert set with, at the very least, their property name, property address, full name, spouse or significant other's name, children's names, you name it. For a business owner, this tool is invaluable. It will help you stay on top of any and all chatter in the social media realm related to your property. It is like a virtual assistant of sorts.

Realize this: You will get positive feedback as well. So, when you do, show your charm and thank your former residents for being great customers and an asset to the community. Develop a quick, witty response that thanks them for their stay and encourages them to come back if things do not work out where they currently live. Heck, ask them to send their friends while they are at it. Your property, your personality and your message.

INVESTOR PROFILE

Name: Rick

Prior Occupation: Pharmacist

Started Investing at Age: 28

First Investment: My wife and I purchased a duplex and rented the other unit out to a friend. This paid our mortgage at the time.

Current Real Estate Holdings: Over 200 units

Why Real Estate: Comfort through cash flow, physicality and the social interaction with others. Being able to talk to current and prospective residents, vendors, employees and others in the industry is a part of the job that I find enjoyable.

I Wish I Knew When I Started That: Partnering with family-members has made me very successful. I wish that I had started earlier on in my career. It is also important to continually reinvest in your properties to prevent deferred maintenance and significant maintenance later on down the line. Keeping your properties well-maintained can help to preserve and keep your property values up as well.

What I Look For in an Investment: Cash flow has always been the main thing I look for. I want to see immediate positive cash flow with strong future growth potential.

To Those Starting Out, I Say: Never sell! Start small, find like-minded partners and amass your holdings. Use your friends and family to increase or enhance your buying power. Get started as early as you can and do not stop!

CHAPTER 19:

The Turnover

"Certain things, they should stay the way they are. You ought to be able to stick them in one of those big glass cases and just leave them alone."

J.D. SALINGER

It happens to the best of us. That is, one of our tenants gives us notice that they will be vacating their apartment home. We take it personally. We grow frustrated. But it's all part of the business. Get used to it. You will need to respond quickly. Yes, immediately your work to both save and make money begins. We will now discuss the efficient way to do things; that is, how to minimize your downtime and quickly restore the income stream generated by the property.

First Things First

Upon receipt of the letter, email or other notice that your good, rent-paying resident is going to vacate or intends to vacate, personally call your residents to see if there is anything that you can do to keep them. If there is a simple situation that can be accommodated or a minimal adjustment to their rent or perhaps a one-time discount, you should always consider it. Always try this first. I cannot tell you how many residents I have kept by just being sensitive to their needs. Always ask. ALWAYS ASK!

Now, if you determine that there is nothing that can be done to avoid the move-out, you should immediately send the resident a letter clarifying your receipt of their notice to vacate and a set of three dates/times you can walk the unit with them to assist in helping them get as much of their security deposit back as possible. Different states have different laws regarding the return of a security deposit, but California requires the deposit and or an accounting of it be returned within 21 days of a resident vacating. In my experience, it is always better to answer questions regarding the security deposit before rather than after you send it back. Generally, the questions you get after you send back the deposit will be frustrated and shocked that you charged for carpet or paint. So take pictures, keep invoices and do the right thing. More below.

And Then What?

Once the tenant confirms with you the date and time of your appointment to walk the apartment home, be sure to take a clipboard, measuring tape and camera to help with pre-ordering supplies, pricing out materials and further determining what work needs to be done. If you determine that there is minimal work that needs to be done, you are ready to schedule the appropriate vendors.

Room for Change

Now, just what vendors are necessary during a turnover? It depends on the unit and the amount of work that is necessary. If there is minimal work, a unit can need as little as a full cleaning and carpet shampoo along with a re-key. In this case, we would only need a handyman or locksmith to change the locks or re-key the unit (do this on every turnover, regardless of whether or not your local law says you have to or not) and a cleaning crew to do the cleanup.

Refer to the pre-agreed-upon prices we learned about earlier on and contact your vendors to schedule them for the soonest time possible after the residents have vacated. When done correctly, this resembles the domino effect. Step by step, the items are completed neatly and in a timely manner. All the while, this helps to ensure minimal downtime and thus enables you to market the unit for rent sooner. You want to hit the ground running once the resident vacates, so plan on scheduling your contractors ahead of time. As soon as you get the keys, get the vendor into the unit to start working. As a best practice, you will likely want to put the unit on a lockbox so that vendors can come and go. Just make sure that you re-key the lock before the new resident moves in so that you are absolutely certain no one else has a key.

To Show or Not to Show?

Generate your advertising and ensure that you maximize your exposure to the public prior to the unit actually being ready. Why? You have the edge from the get-go. Create your hype by using words and expressions like "this one won't last," "these rarely come available," etc. When paired with the right pricing, and pricing is key, you will not have vacancies for long.

Just like we want to turn over our apartment home as quickly as possible, we also want to show the unit to prospective residents as quickly as possible. And although we want to maximize our income, remember that depending on the living situation of your current resident, attempting to pre-lease the unit by showing the current space to prospects may or may not be advisable. Use your own judgment here. Additionally, make sure that your lease has a clause that allows you to pre-market the space based upon mutual agreed upon terms between you and your current resident. Although you want to pre-lease, remember, it is still someone's home. Be kind and courteous to your residents. More importantly, be considerate and compassionate.

If you are showing the apartment home to prospective residents, you will want to establish a policy of pre-qualifying the prospects so as to deter just anyone from entering into a currently occupied apartment home. You never know just who you are dealing with when a call comes in. So be smart and pre-qualify the prospect. Follow Fair Housing protocol as well. What you do for one prospect, you must do for all prospects. Steer clear of any potential discrimination claims. If you are going to show the unit, show the unit. If not, don't show it until the unit is vacant, turned over and ready to show. It's your choice. You decide.

One of the very best practices that you can follow is the act of not showing an apartment home that is in the process of being turned over. If you show it before (like we discussed), that's fine. However, with tools, debris and other items in the middle of a job-site or disaster zone as contractors are working on preparing the vacant space for rent, just from a liability perspective, you will want to avoid showing the unit. All it takes is one slip and fall and you can end up with an insurance claim, or even worse, a lawsuit. Don't set yourself up to be sued. Avoid liability by pro-actively seeking to or looking prevent it.

C H A P T E R   2 0 :

Collecting the Rent

*"Service to others is the rent you pay
for your room here on Earth."*

MUHAMMAD ALI

Once an apartment home has been rented, the fun has officially
begun. The fun, as us landlords know it, is collecting the rent. That
is, reaping the benefits of our industrious venture into financial well-
being. Although it seems simple, collecting rent is a task that requires
strategic skill and planning on your behalf. But with the right plan, you
will make it easier not only on yourself but also on your residents. Just
as when you want to buy groceries, you walk into grocery store, collect
your items and pay the cashier, your residents have received a service
and need to pay you for the service. Make it as simple as possible for
your residents to pay you. Here is how we do this.

The System

The first of the month comes, and it's like clockwork. Rent is due. What
you will likely find is that many of your residents do not have savings
accounts with significant balances. What's more, the check that your
residents pay to you for their rent is likely the biggest expense they
have for the month. While that should make it all the easier for them
to remember to pay, they also realize that if they forego paying their

rent they can buy nice things or waste their money without having to honor their obligation to pay rent.

So, around the 18th of the month (for the following month) you are going to send your resident an envelope with an invoice for the rental amount due. On this invoice you will remind them that their rent is due on the first and late thereafter. Therefore, they are subject to the late penalties and now possibly face the dilemma of having to pay by cashier's check or money order only. But in the meantime, so long as rent is paid on time, you can accept personal check, cashier's check or money order. Cash is never an option. You are not a grocery store. You are a business that thrives on books, records and documentable, verifiable income. As such, cash is unacceptable.

You can use Quickbooks, On-Site, Yardi or a simple spreadsheet to log the receipt of income and accurately credit the resident who paid. Once complete, print what is known as a rent roll or an aged receivable report that shows who has not paid rent and who owes a balance. From there, you can proceed to follow up with this resident and find out when you will receive the rent. Of course, there are notices and documents that need to be posted in conjunction with this conversation, but a conversation always helps things to go over smoother. Don't you feel better when someone talks to you first?

If, Then

It's bound to happen at one time or another. Your resident will be late or have some sort of sob story as to why they can't pay their rent. These range from the sad ("My child is sick") to the average ("I'm really having hard time") to the understood ("I lost my job") to the unacceptable ("You see that big flat-screen television box by the dumpster? Well, I bought that with my rent money."). You always post on their door your three-day notice to pay rent or quit in accordance with the timeframe spelled out in your lease agreement. Again, I cannot stress to you how important it is for you to have a verbal conversation in addition to posting this notice, possibly doing so before or as you post the notice. Posting a notice is like dropping a bomb. If you talk to your resident, you can diffuse the situation. If you just leave it on their door, it's bound to explode. So, what do you do? Talk to them and walk them through it. This is not rocket science, people. It's apartment management. When all else fails, employ common sense.

After you have posted notice and you have communicated with your residents, you will want to establish an understanding of whether or not they can pay their rent on this later date. If the date is acceptable to you and you will be accepting their payment, then you hold on to the three-day notice and let them know that if they do not pay, you will be sending them to the attorney's office for eviction. You also have the ability to simply deny the resident's request, which is often advisable if the resident is otherwise a nuisance or cause of problems.

If you decide that you do not want to accept the rent, you will want to refuse any payments from the resident and advise them to contact your law firm with any questions or concerns about the pending lawsuit. The eviction process can take between 25 and 45 days, depending on the state where your property is located. This means that in some cases a resident may in fact have time to come up with the money that is necessary for them to stay at the property. If not, do not feel bad. Realize that despite the unfortunate circumstances, this is in fact a business agreement that was not honored by the other party.

Don't focus on the eviction; focus on the work that will be necessary to get the apartment home rent ready and leased.

INVESTOR PROFILE

Name: John

Prior Occupation: Student

Started Investing at Age: 15

First Investment: 22 units that I purchased with my dad.

Current Real Estate Holdings: 500 + multifamily units, 400K + Square feet of office space, self-storage, farmland and ground leases. A diverse but fun portfolio!

Why Real Estate: Its physicality provides comfort. Aside from the physicality, it holds its value. Stability through quantity is another point There is also more stability in having multiple units versus just one rental house or one of another property type.

I Wish I Knew When I Started That: Paying down a loan early can have a significant impact on your cash flow. Sure, it might have more of an adverse impact on your cash flow for the first five years or so, but afterwards, your return can increase greatly. It is also important to build your reserves in case of emergency. Things come up in the course of owning and operating real estate

What I Look For in an Investment: From a physical perspective, I like good locations, not too old, nice property in a good location is ideal. No negative cash flow going in. I need to make money day one!

To Those Starting Out, I Say: Don't overleverage yourself, use financing conservatively. You can get yourself into trouble and compromise your operation by overleveraging. Next, the acquisition of existing apartments can be better than developing your own units, but in any case, as an operator you will want to push rents to off-set rising costs. Visit your properties often and do not be an absentee owner.

If You Can't Beat 'Em, Hire 'Em!

"The ultimate victory in competition is derived from the inner satisfaction of knowing that you have done your best and that you have gotten the most out of what you had to give."

HOWARD COSELL

You've had it. You're done. Whether or not you've followed the directions I've given on how to manage your multifamily investment easily and efficiently, you just do not want to do it. That's fine. Not everyone is cut out for property management. Really. It's true. It is a simple task on the surface, but there is a lot to it. There are multiple facets. That is, multiple tasks to be completed within the primary task and then there are more minute and yet significant tasks to be completed within those tasks. You see, there is a reason that people make a living managing property. It is a unique niche within the commercial real estate industry, and there are a number of professionals who would like to help you with your commercial real estate investments. And now that you have some experience and can appreciate the monotony (yes, I said it) and the grind that is property management, you will have more of an appreciation for the company that you hire to manage your assets for you.

But just how do you hire a property management company? Sure, it's much like the hiring of any other vendor or service provider that you work with, but it's also different in that this is not only a niche within the real estate industry but also a niche within the finance industry. Within this overlay lies the ability to manage the physical asset but also to manage the financial asset. The unique, synergistic relationship should not be underestimated. Think about it: you tried and could not continue. And since you could not continue, you will need to hire a company that can protect your interests on-site, protect your investment, minimize your liability on-site and add value to your investment. But just how do you do it? How do you qualify which management companies are best suited to manage your property? It all starts through the education and information process. Let's go.

Education & Information

The property-management business is quite competitive. You see, management accounts or management business generally change hands on the sale of property or if an individual owner is unhappy or unsatisfied with their current arrangement. As you can imagine, this does not happen often. So, when you call around and do your first bit of due diligence on the potential management companies that you will be interviewing, expect some enthusiasm. But where should you start? There are likely dozens of companies within the market area of your real estate holdings, and you do not want to waste your time interviewing each and every company within your market.

Start by asking the broker who sold you the building if he has any recommendation for a professional management company within the market area of the subject property. It is likely that the broker will have at least two referrals for potential management companies. Add these two potential candidates to your list. Next, log on to the Institute of Real Estate Management's website, and do a simple search yourself. Located at (http://www.irem.org/), the Institute of Real Estate Management (IREM) is the commercial real estate management arm of the

National Association of Realtors. Together, these two organizations represent and educate more commercial real estate professionals than any other organization in the world. They offer not only an individual designation known as the Certified Property Manager designation, but also a designation or accreditation at the company level. There is a directory on the IREM website that This designation or accreditation, the Accredited Management Organization, is held only by those real estate management companies who have passed a third-party evaluation of their financials, insurance coverage and other important paperwork such as lease and management agreements. So add one, two or three company names to your list, and be ready to schedule an interview appointment with each company.

Your initial meeting with the potential management company should take place in the candidate's office and should answer for you several primary questions and a host of secondary questions. From your first telephone call or email to the potential management company, you should begin your judgment or assessment of whether or not their level of professionalism and customer service will work with your goals of ownership. Did they respond quickly to your questions or concerns? Did you wait for a response for an extended period of time? This is important to know and important to log in your notes. If the company is eager to meet with you to uncover your needs and your concerns, you could be on to something. In any case, reserve your judgment or your decision until after you have met with the candidate.

Before your meeting you will also want to conduct Due Diligence 2013. Yes, you guessed it. Due diligence in today's day in age is comprised of a Google search. So, Google the property management company that you will be meeting with. What is their message? What do they have to say? What is their company voice? Read about the principals and understand their principles. Do they have any negative reviews online or scathing feedback from a client or irritated tenants that could possibly carry over into the operation and management of your property? While you should realize that anyone can sign on to the Internet and post negative reviews or negative feedback, anonymously no less, it is important to identify patterns of such reviews. If you see a lot of it, be prepared to ask the company about it at your meeting. If they do not have an explanation, you will probably want to look for a new company. Having done your due diligence ahead of the meeting, it is now time to arrange the meeting with the appropriate personnel or key contacts at the respective firms you will be interviewing. Make sure you get to meet everyone, not just the founder or principal.

Who Should Be There?

There is a plethora of questions that you can ask and will ask during the course of interviewing potential management companies. While there are specific items that you will want to find out during the course of your interview, a good portion of the interview is just like any other interview in that you are trying to find out whether or not it seems like a good fit. You will know right off the bat with whom you get along and with whom you do not. It is important to ensure that anyone involved with the management of your assets will be present during the meeting. If there is a regional manager, a vice president, a director of property management or any other operational personnel that will be involved in the day-to-day management duties, you will want to ensure that they are present and that you can also get along with and see yourself working with them. The resident manager need not be present, but it will be a good idea for you to meet the resident manager prior to hiring the management company.

With the roster of attendees set, you will now begin to craft your list of questions. The idea is for you to understand whether or not the management company can be of assistance to you as well as become familiar with their company structure, their experience, their expertise, their niche and their financial reporting capabilities. But before you meet with the company and before you discuss with them your concerns, it is a good idea for you to request the addresses of the three properties in the firm's portfolio that are closest to your property, and walk those properties. At the very least, you should drive by those properties to visualize their work-in-progress. That is, look for cleanliness, upkeep and signs that the lights are on and someone is home. Meaning, there are signs advertising any vacancies, and the resident manager's telephone number is prominently displayed. Having done your due diligence, you are now ready to begin the interview process.

What to Say

Open the discussion by informing the management company of the reason behind your acquisition. Explain to them that you bought the property to help pay for your children's college tuition or that you purchased the property to help supplement your income. It is important to inform the management company of your goals of ownership. Telling them a bit about yourself and gauging their reaction will tell you something about them as well. You will also want to learn about their management style and how they handle things. Who will be involved with the portfolio? What is their experience? For how long have they been managing real estate? What is their experience with this particular asset class? Do they know the market? Where do they see rents headed?

How do they market vacant units for rent? Do they charge any additional fees for their marketing and leasing? Is their management fee all-inclusive? How much do they charge to manage a property of this size? Are they insured as a company? Are you indemnified and held harmless from any claims resulting from their negligence? You get the gist. This is an interview. This is an interview in which you can dictate the terms, control the flow and ask any questions that you would like. Ask to see sample financial reports from a few of the properties in the firm's portfolio. Can you easily understand them? Do not feel embarrassed or ashamed to ask questions. You are the one making the decision, and you should feel comfortable with the arrangement.

Just like the rental activity, marketing and leasing strategies are significant to income, so is the maintenance activity to the overall operation and profitability of a particular management arrangement. How does the firm handle maintenance? Do they contract with outside vendors or do they handle maintenance (or a large portion of it) in house? If so, do they mark up the maintenance expense to profit off of it? Or do they bill the expense back to the property at cost (not profiting off of it)? While contacting outside vendors can result in a decreased maintenance expense on occasion, it can also result in an increased maintenance expense and decreased customer satisfaction due to long waits for service providers. Remember, you are in a service business, so understand how the management company plans to keep your residents happy.

Next, it is a good idea to ask whether the firm's portfolio consists mostly of fee-managed properties (those managed for a third party) or self-managed properties (those owned by the firm or the firm's principals). While you can argue for or against either, what you are most interested in is how the firm cares for the properties it manages. Often times, a firm whose portfolio consists mostly of self-managed properties will be better kept. A firm who simply relies on fee-management can be more astute or quick to respond in that their business exists solely as a result of the ongoing patronage of the property owner. This is similar to the "You say jump, I ask, 'How high?'" mentality. Realize that not every company you meet with will take this approach to the management of your property. So, when you encounter this hesitation or lack of cooperation, cross the company off of your list. There are too many companies out there who want your business.

Also during the interview process, you will want to find out just how much experience the management firm has in dealing with your specific property type. If the firm manages mostly office or industrial properties, they may not be the best fit for an apartment building. On the other hand, if the firm has a wealth of experience with apartments, and you are looking for someone to manage a multi-tenant industrial park or office building, perhaps their strengths or experience would make them a qualified candidate. Probe more in detail about the principals' track record and inquire as to whether or not any of the team has hands-on experience managing this type of property. You need to know this before you make your decision.

Before you leave the interview, ask for a sample management agreement, an insurance certificate showing that the firm maintains either general or professional liability or both, and a list of three current clients for which the firm manages. Inform the company that you would like to contact these clients to discuss the professional services that they provide and the level of personal care and attention that they receive from the firm.

Another bit of information that you will want to collect during the interview process is the state licensing information by each of the key personnel assigned to the account. Ensure that the firm is licensed with the state's Real Estate Commission or Department of Real Estate and that the personnel who will be working with you have clean license histories. You can independently verify this information on the websites of most state agencies. If someone has an expired license, you will want to show them that you know of the expiration and ask when they plan to renew the license. On the other hand, if the principal's license was revoked or rescinded for any number of reasons, you should probably steer clear of the company. There are plenty of other options in the world of real estate management. I mean really, could you ever live it down if you hired a company who ended up stealing money from you? Chances are no, especially if you noticed the questionable track record before you hired the company.

After you have interviewed at least three companies, put your data into a spreadsheet that will allow you to compare the pros and cons of each company's proposal easily. If you encounter a question or subject matter during one of your interviews that did not come up in another, then telephone or email the other management companies to clarify their stance or their opinion. Once you have all of your information compiled into a neat and orderly spreadsheet, you are ready to make a decision, or at the very least, decide on the top two choices to then meet with them again.

At the final interview, you will want to clarify terms of your working agreement. If there is anything you heard, misheard or perhaps misinterpreted, make it a point to clarify it during the second interview. By this time, you should have established some sort of a professional rapport with the prospective company, and you will better understand whether or not this is a company with which you could see yourself doing business.

One last thing you will want to review is the management company's protocol for notifying the current residents of the change in management. The sooner this is done, the better. Of course, once the residents have the new company's information, they are less inclined to bother you, right? True to an extent, but you always want to be available for residents should they have a valid concern regarding the management company.

One more important aspect of the interview will be to understand the company's primary course of business. Are they a brokerage that also manages property? Are they just a management company? Or are they a full-service real estate investment company that owns, brokers and manages real estate? In business, opinions and advice are important. And if you are doing business with someone who stands to profit greatly off of a sale, or only stands to make money if you continue to own the property, you are not getting impartial advice. For the best advice and perhaps the best solution, opt for the full-service real estate investment firm. After the full-service firm, then consider the real estate management firm. Real estate brokers who broker full-time simply do not belong in real estate management. It is a specialized business with too many rules, regulations and frequent changes with which to keep up. If you are looking for someone to truly minimize your headaches and liabilities, you want to entrust your assets upon a true professional, one who will create value in your working relationship. Your property should not just be seen as a management account that creates a steady paycheck for an otherwise full-time real estate broker. Brokers serve their purpose in our investment cycles, and that is in bringing us deals to underwrite and acquire.

Immediately following your second meeting with the management company, you will want to send the management agreement from the company that you will likely be signing with to your business law or contract attorney. Ensure that you are adequately protected and or indemnified under the contract. Do not hesitate to have your attorney mark-up, edit, review or revise the document. If the prospective management company does not agree, find out from your attorney what and why they are in disagreement and what the specific clause does to protect you. Is it absolutely necessary? If so, you may have to work on the management company or otherwise notify them that this verbiage is absolutely required in order to protect your interests as the owner. If the company wants to do business with you, they will figure out a way to make it happen. Or, their attorney will figure out some sort of verbiage that makes the contract work for them. I am always amazed by the apartment owner who sees no need to have an attorney evaluate their management agreement. Here you are entrusting a firm you with which have never done business with a million-dollar asset and thousands in periodic cash flow. You won't spend $500 on an attorney's time to review a document? Come on.

Regardless of how much you like the company, you should always stay away from fixed-term contracts. No vendor, no matter how good, is worth more than a 30-day contract with a 30-day option to cancel—that is, a 30-day notice to cancel the contract and hire a new company. In the rare event that things go sideways and you just cannot get along with the company or its personnel, you will want to get them out as soon as possible. Make sure they are amiable to these terms. Think about it: would you want to do business with someone who was inappreciative or unhappy with you? Probably not. You should realize that having done the work yourself, property management is not a particularly glamorous business. It is a service business that places a heavy emphasis on service. Property owners have a tendency to underestimate the level of service that is required, while in turn hammering down on the management company to minimize vacancy rates and minimize expenses. If it were that easy, you would manage your real estate holdings yourself! So be compassionate, be pro-active and be aware.

Now that you are less involved in the actual operation of the property, you can be more involved in the financial aspect of the operation, otherwise known as **asset management**. While asset management is the more sophisticated side of property management, an astute property- management company will be well aware of the significance of a property's financial performance. As asset manager, you will look at rental trends, evaluate the occupancy rates of your property and those of neighboring properties and the sub-market as whole in the hopes of identifying upside potential to increase your rents and thus increase revenue. The good thing about this scenario is that if you are a bit overzealous in your projects, a respectable management company will alert you to the fact. However, you may encounter a situation in which the management company keeps rents lower than market. This is worthy of a sit-down meeting to discuss. Equally important is the upward trending of expenses or rent-ready apartment homes sitting vacant for extended periods of time. While this is part of the business, it is important to let the management company know that you are aware of the issue and that you are not happy about it.

Throughout this book, over and over, we have discussed that real estate is not so much about location, location, location as it is about the art of relationships. Knowing and being aligned with the right people will help you enjoy greater success in your investment career. Having grown up in the real estate business, I cannot tell you how many times an investor who worked with my dad had made a comment to me along the lines of, "Your father did so much for me just off a handshake." And that's the type of guy my dad is. But things have changed, and we have transitioned from the handshake era to the contract era. Terms may have changed, but people don't. Being able to delegate and trust those working on your behalf provides an unparalleled peace of mind. So long as you do your homework ahead of time and closely follow along at home, you will be comfortable and on your way to making additional successful investments.

NICHOLAS A. DUNLAP

CHAPTER 22:

The Brick-and-Mortar Piggy Bank

"It's tangible. It's solid. It's beautiful. It's artistic, from my standpoint, and I just love real estate."

DONALD TRUMP

Real estate investing is not easy. It may not be overly complicated to understand, but it is an industry that is multi-faceted and constantly changing. Markets are diverse and require an expert insight into unique and subtle nuances that separate neighborhoods, cities, counties and states. There is no one-size-fits-all approach to investing. Many investors have lost their life savings "winging it" or using the "shotgun" approach. Refine your approach to investing. You see, one of the biggest mistakes that individual owners make when managing their property or portfolio is attempting to run before they can walk. Although there are no specific requirements, licenses or certifications required to manage a property that you own, there are certain policies and procedures that absolutely must be adhered to or followed. Many times, a new owner will acquire a property and attempt to recreate the wheel, only to find that in recreating the wheel, they have put themselves in the red financially. There is no shame in following a tried, true system, especially when it leads you down a path of success.

Start conservatively. Before you venture off into the world of projected income and appreciation, start with a bread-and-butter investment. That is, start with something small and simple that makes money. If you have the financial wherewithal to acquire a larger property, that's fine; just be sure to align yourself with the right management company. You see, in real estate, in business and in life, people have a tendency to bite off more than they can chew. Making the wrong investment can be the biggest bite a person can take. The headaches, nightmares and frustrations of a negative cash flowing piece of real estate can drive even the most intelligent investors insane. So don't be in a hurry. Don't rush. Take your time, and realize that you will be strategically amassing your wealth in a method in which you can continue to grow and leverage your existing assets into additional holdings. It takes patience and it takes common sense (or uncommon sense, depending on how you look at it).

Quick and logical thinking will enable you to move mountains when you are dealing with what can often seem like minutiae. Focusing on the big picture without overlooking the details of your transaction, be it the smallest of numbers in your spreadsheet or the terms you are seeking in the negotiation of your new acquisition, can be the difference between a cash cow and a dead duck. So, take the time to develop a strong foundation before putting on the decorative finish. It is more important to understand the operations or systems behind the successful function of an apartment building than it is simply to purchase a building and raise rents to increase your income.

Understand the fundamentals, and become comfortable with the different cost and investment measures. Talk to brokers and impress them with your newfound knowledge of these key terms and phrases. Master the marke,t and opine on prices, rents and where you see the market headed. If you live, breathe and eat commercial real estate, the art of investing will slowly but surely become second nature to you. Along the way, you will impress some people and improve your own understanding of things, but more importantly, you will demonstrate to yourself firsthand that you can do it. You can be a successful real estate investor, owner or operator. You just need to put in the work FIRST.

So, understand that it is not easy, but through a sound, conservative approach to investing, effective planning and management of your property, you can not only succeed, but thrive. And whether you just own or both own and manage your own properties, you will come to realize the direct effect your efforts can have on your bottom line. Everything from pricing out projects and diligence in competitive bidding to utility-expense management can have a significant impact on your cash flow and impact your return on investment. If you put in the work and take the time to understand the market, understand your property and truly focus on its operations, you are bound for success.

Compare yourself to a chef in the kitchen. Using a pre-established location with pre-existing ingredients, you enter into the mix and put everything together to arrive at your own recipe. When done right, this recipe should please your customers and keep them coming back for more. As a landlord, you are the chef. Once you have found your recipe for success, do not change a thing. You see, as long as there has been real estate, there has been the need for real estate management. It might not be easy, and you may find yourself working harder than you would have hoped to on a second job or part-time project, but it is a true path to building and preserving your wealth through real, tangible assets.

So, as you go forward, remember to think intelligently when you purchase your property. Do not overleverage, and instead proceed with caution. Pursue cash flow, and remember that while projections are great, nothing beats current cash flow. So, follow the steps for success, and plan your goals of ownership. Continue to monitor and manage these goals as you operate your property. Keep exceptional records, and be courteous to your residents, vendors and staff. If you do this and are successful, you will likely be implementing your own brand of management on another property somewhere down the line.

If you implement the right systems, your biggest obstacle will not be in finding or sourcing the capital to invest; it will be in locating the right investment opportunities for your portfolio. With the right relationships in place, it is simply a matter of looking at and underwriting as many opportunities as come your way in order to find the one perfect match. That match is not made of straw because that would be too easy. It is not made out of sticks, which are stronger than straw. No, your match is made out of bricks. Bricks and mortar, to be exact. In the world of investing, there are few stronger assets than brick and mortar. Now it's time to turn yours into a piggy bank.

INVESTOR PROFILE

Name: Bob

Prior Occupation: Bank Auditor

Started Investing at Age: 24

First Investment: Rental house

Current Real Estate Holdings: A mixed portfolio of apartment, condominiums and office buildings valued in excess of $95,000,000

Why Real Estate: It's solid, dynamic, reliable and trustworthy with a heavy emphasis on its physicality as an asset class.

I Wish I Knew When I Started That: Be frugal and save your cash to invest.

What I Look For in an Investment: The old cliché "location, location, location" is true not just in residential real estate but also when it comes to identifying a prime investment opportunity in commercial real estate as well. Aside from an asset's location, the financial return it generates also weighs heavily in determining the overall value of an investment opportunity.

To Those Starting Out, I Say: Be diligent and be focused. Know your markets and have the capital on-hand to be nimble and move swiftly on the opportunities that you discover.

NICHOLAS A. DUNLAP

Investor's Toolbox:
Terms, Tips & Tricks

Checklists and Step-by-Steps for the Successful Landlord

Terms

After Tax Cash Flow: Income left over after the payment of income taxes.

Annual Debt Service: Loan or mortgage payments annualized.

Before Tax Cash Flow: Periodic income received by the investor after paying all operating expenses and the loan payment.

Capitalization Rate: The relationship or ratio between the Net Operating Income of a property and its market value, also known as the yield, if you were to pay all cash for the asset. To arrive at the cap rate, you divide the net operating income by the market value.

Cash-on-Cash Rate of Return: The rate of return measuring the before tax cash flow return to investors on the total cash invested. To arrive at the cash-on-cash or $/$%, you divide the annual before-tax cash flow by the initial investment.

Cost Per Square Foot: The cost measure summarizing the dollar value per square foot of the subject property. To arrive at the cost per square foot, you will divide the cost or market price by the total square footage of the improvements.

Cost Per Unit: Also known as the cost per door or cost per key, the cost per unit represents the per-unit sales price of a property. To arrive at the cost per unit, you simply divide the purchase price by the total number of units at the property.

Debt Coverage Ratio: Simply put, the debt coverage ratio represents the availability of income generated by the property to pay for the loan. To arrive at the debt service, you will divide the annual income generated by a property by the annual debt service.

Down payment: Your initial equity; your out-of-pocket capital outlay into your investment. This represents the total amount of money that you have invested upon acquisition and will serve as the baseline measurement for any of your investment measures.

Effective Gross Income: The actual gross income received; this includes all rent and other sources of income collected at the property. This measurement can either be cash or accrual based in that the term "effective" refers only to the income collected.

Equity: Dollar amount representing the ownership interest by a person in an asset. This can be either positive in that the measure is favorable or has increased over the course of ownership or negative in that the interest actually decreased in value.

Estoppels Certificates: A document designed to give a third party (buyer/lender/appraiser) information on the arrangement or business agreement between the landlord and tenant.

Exchange (1031): A tax-deferred exchange that allows for the seller of a property to identify three properties of equal to or greater than values of the property being sold and close escrow within a limited period of time while not pocketing any of the proceeds in order to defer taxes and maintain a low basis in the newly acquired properties.

Gross Income: The total income generated by a property.

Gross Income Multiplier: A ratio used to compare the total income collected by a property to its market value. To arrive at the gross income multiplier or GIM, simply divide the market value by the gross income.

Gross Rent Multiplier: A ratio used to compare the total rental income collected by a property to its market value. To arrive at the gross rent multiplier or GRM, simply divide the market value by the gross rental income.

Internal Rate of Return: The annualized, effective rate of return generated by the asset. This is a complex investment measure, and although useful, it is a sophisticated measure relied upon by private equity and other such institutional investors. Step up your game.

Loss to Lease: The difference between current lease rates and those of market; this measurement describes the landlord's total losses due to existing lease terms.

Loss Runs: An insurance term referring to a report that details any losses or claims that have occurred at a property within a given time period.

Net Operating Income: The operating income leftover after the operating expenses have been paid but before the debt service has been paid. EGI-OP EX = NOI (Net Operating Income).

Occupancy Rate: The percentage rate of occupied apartments or space at an apartment or office building. To arrive at the occupancy rate, divide the number of occupied units by the total number of units.

Operating Expenses: The total dollar amount of expenses incurred through the operation of property. This does not include debt service.

Pro-forma: Pro-form refers to projected or otherwise not actual numbers. The term pro-forma also refers to a setup sheet or marketing package often prepared by real estate brokers that includes projected numbers.

Rent Roll: A list that summarizes by number each apartment home, the corresponding resident and the amount paid in rent on a monthly basis. In some instances, this report will also summarize additional fees paid on a monthly basis as well, i.e., pet rent, garage rent or utilities.

Return on Investment: See also **Cash-on-Cash Rate of Return**. The return on investment or ROI illustrates the percentage rate of return on a particular investment. To arrive at the ROI, you divide your initial investment by the before-tax cash flow.

Unit Mix: The total number of units and their corresponding unit types; generally given when summarizing the property as a whole.

Unit Type: The floor-plan or setup of unit; this refers to the bed and bath count of a particular unit.

Vacancy Rate: The percentage rate representing the number of units or space that is vacant. To arrive at the vacancy rate, simply divide the number of vacant units by the total number of units. The vacancy rate plus the occupancy rate should always equal 100%.

Tips and Tricks

As you become familiar with your tenants, your property and your cash flow, you will notice hiccups or hitches in your operation that can be streamlined or improved. Identify and embrace them as improvements that should be made. Do not simply ignore them; that will do nothing for you or your investment. While there will be certain aspects of your operation that are unique to your property, there are others that are the same across the board. This makes it easy for you to observe and implement what works for other successful landlords.

Consider the following tips in operating your property so that you build off of others' successes instead of delaying your own.

Automate

Regardless of your skill level, it is important to stay abreast of the newest technologies as they relate to business. Property management is no different. Due to the robotic nature of many management-related duties and tasks, you might find that it is worth it for you to implement these online systems to help automate your property-management tasks. Conducting a simple cost/benefit analysis of your time versus your expenditure on key systems to help streamline the day-to-management may reveal that you would greatly benefit from these systems.

Tenant portals, online rent payment and additional tenant interface and correspondence can be facilitated via pre-set and automated systems. If you consider yourself to be capable and can afford the expense, I highly recommend that you maintain an automated technological platform. This will help you as you make additional investments and seek to maintain the same quality of ownership and management.

Bi-annual Checks

Every year, on at least two occasions you should provide your residents with adequate notice and proceed to gain access to their apartment so that you can check to ensure that their smoke detectors are working properly. While you are at it, you should also check the angle stops and ball valves underneath the sinks to ensure there are no leaks or damages being caused. Last but not least, look for any utilities that might be being abused: water constantly running or faucets dripping so heavily that it appears the faucet is turned on.

Preventative maintenance is almost always less costly than the over-looked items that will grow into big issues. So, keep your eyes open and use these inspections as an opportunity to preserve your NOI.

Care

If you do not care about your property or your tenants, then hire someone who does. Failing to pay attention to the needs of your customers does no good for anyone. Develop and utilize a move-in survey and an exit interview to figure out: why someone moved in and what their experience was like, why they are moving and what they wish would have been different. A little bit of caring goes a long way. Remember, although it is a business, human nature prevails above all.

Take Pictures

If you have come to understand one thing during the course of reading this book, it should be that your records are of the utmost importance. And what better method of documentation than photographs? Before and after a resident moves into an apartment home, it is important to take pictures to accompany the checklist of conditions that is typically signed by the residents upon move-in and kept with the lease agreement.

Should a dispute arise, having pictures on hand to substantiate any charges or tenant-perceived discrepancies will greatly assist in minimizing headaches due to haggling residents.

Create Income

Your income property is just that: income producing your property. Whether you have purchased an apartment complex or an office building, there are a number of ways for you to maximize the income streams associated with your investment. Let's start with your apartment property.

Your tenants should pay you rent, pet rent, late fees, rent for storages, rent for garages, rent for additional parking spaces, etc. You can build the fees (with the exception of the late fee) into the rent or you can break them down separately. In addition, you can evaluate the marketplace and establish an understanding of whether or not other property owners are forcing the tenants to pay their utilities. Ideally, your tenant will pay these expenses (gas, water, trash, electricity), thus removing the burden of utility expenses from your operating statement. Regardless of your property size, billing back the utilities to residents is an excellent way to improve your bottom line.

Partnerships are another great way to increase your income. Cable television companies such as AT&T, Direct TV and Time Warner Cable offer programs where they will share with you a percentage of the income they generate at your property. They should provide you with not only an ongoing commission, but also a generous upfront bonus. Be sure to review the contract, and if all looks good, sign it.

Just like the cable TV companies, laundry companies also provide upfront bonuses and ongoing commissions depending on the agreement you have worked out. Be sure to obtain multiple proposals and bid the service contracts obtained by each vendor against the other. You can do the same on renter's insurance as well.

Vending machines can also be a great source of income. Whether you are selling soda pop, candy bars and snacks that will save your residents a trip to the store, or laundry detergent and other laundry items, you can pull in good money simply from having these machines on site. Talk to Pepsi and Coca-Cola, and then consider buying your own machines before you proceed. Pepsi and Coke will often provide an upfront bonus and a smaller ongoing percentage share of income, but you will not have to service the machines yourself which can be time consuming.

The aforementioned suggestions should be scrutinized, evaluated and closely considered before you implement or institute them across your portfolio. While you always want to maximize your income, you want to be sure that the proposed partnership or working agreement is a good fit for you. Remember, as you meet people and become more involved in the apartment industry, you will realize that there are certain programs that will or will not work for you. Embrace those things that will.

The Ten #BMPB Commandments of CRE Investment

1. Know your markets: rental and for sale.
2. Assemble a team of trustworthy, accomplished and experienced professionals to advise you and consult with on investments.

3. Spend at least 30 minutes a day browsing the market and underwriting potential acquisitions.

4. Use OPM (Other People's Money) to your benefit. Be smart with leverage.

5. You make your money when you buy, so buy smart.

6. Cash flow is king.

7. It's not just location; it's location, then numbers, then customer relations.

8. Always be prepared to move on the opportunities available in the marketplace.

9. Know when to walk away from a potential acquisition.

10. Don't sell unless you have to or will significantly increase the return on your current investment.

The #BMPB 11-Step Investment Process

1. Understand the type of commercial real estate investment (asset) that you are looking to acquire.

2. Familiarize yourself with the market for this type of property as well as the market for available financing.

3. Identify potential acquisition opportunities.

4. Underwrite potential acquisition opportunities.

5. Submit a Letter of Intent and negotiate terms.

6. Open escrow.

7. Conduct your due diligence.

8. Obtain financing.

9. Close escrow.

10. Notify tenants of change in ownership/management.

11. Assume management.

#BMPB Commercial Real Estate Acquisition Team Roster

Investment Team
Underwriting and Financial Due Diligence

Commercial Real Estate Broker: _____

Lender: _____

Title Representative: _____

Insurance Agent: _____

Property Manager (or Company): _____

Business/Contract Attorney: _____

Real Estate Attorney: _____

Accountant/CPA: _____

Due Diligence Team

Physical and Operational Due Diligence

General Contractor: _____

Roofer: _____

Plumber: _____

Pest Control/Termite: _____

Property Manager (Expert): _____

#BMPB Lease Abstract

Tenant (s) Full Name (on Lease): _____

Registered Occupants (#): _____

Unit Address: _____

Unit Address (Continued): _____

Unit Type: _____

Unit Size (Square footage): _____

Original Lease (To/From) Dates: _____

Original Rent Amount: _____

Original Security Deposit Amount: _____

Current Rent Amount: _____

Current Security Deposit Amount: _____

Resident Paid Utilities: _____

Pets (Y/N): _____

Contact Info:

Tenant Cell #: _____

Tenant Home #: _____

Tenant Work #: _____

Tenant Email: _____

Additional Details: _____

#BMPB Vendor List

Accountant: _____

Appliances:

Purchase/Install: _____

Repair: _____

Architect: _____

Asphalt/Paving: _____

Attorney:

Business/Contract: _____

Employment Law/Labor: _____

Landlord/Tenant: _____

Boiler/Water Heater: _____

Carpet/Flooring: _____

City:

Building Dept: _____

Code Enforcement: _____

Utilities: _____

Cleaning Service: _____

Electrician: _____

Gardener: _____

General Contractor: _____

Haul-away/Special Pickup: _____

HVAC: _____

Insurance Agent: _____

Landscaper: _____

Laundry: _____

Maintenance:

Routine: _____

Turnover/Make Ready: _____

Painter: _____

Pest Control:

Routine Service: _____

Rodent/Other: _____

Termite: _____

Plumber: _____

Clogged Toilets/Sinks: _____

Clogged Lines/Rooter/Slab Leaks _____

Gas Lines/Gas Leaks: _____

Leak Detector: _____

Pool/Spa: _____

Cleaner: _____

Drain Repair: _____

Signage: _____

Supplies: _____

Maintenance: _____

Management: _____

Towing: _____

Utilities: _____

Electricity: _____

Gas: _____

Sewer: _____

Trash: _____

Water: _____

#BMPB Letter of Intent

DATE:

TO:

RE: Non-binding Letter of Intent to Purchase Property:

- Property:
- Purchase Price:
- Payment of Purchase Price:
- Contingency Periods:
- Financing Contingency:
- Close of Escrow:
- Deposits:
- Right to Extend:
- Escrow:
- Title:
- Purchase and Sale Agreement:
- Title:
- Leases and Service Contracts:
- Closing Costs, Credits and Pro-rations:
- Estoppel Certificates:
- Right of Entry:
- Maintenance Obligations:

- Material Changes:
- Assignment:
- Broker Commission:
- Changes to Purchase Agreement:
- Tax Deferred Exchange:

This letter is intended to be a non-binding statement of the terms of a proposed transaction. It is subject to the negotiation, execution and delivery of definitive legal documents by buyer and seller reflecting the terms and conditions set forth in this letter of intent and other customary provisions not addressed in this letter of intent.

By executing and submitting a copy of this letter, Buyer agrees to the above. This offer shall expire at DATE and TIME.

Sincerely,
Buyer

Agreed to and Accepted by:

Buyer: _____

Date: _____

Seller: _____

Date: _____

#BMPB Acquisition Data Form

Listing Price:

Current Loan Terms (if Assumable):

Cost Per Unit:

Cost Per Square Foot:

Cap Rate:

GRM:

Gross Income:

Total Expenses (Current):

Days on Market:

Reason for Selling:

Is the Seller Exchanging:

Has the Seller Identified Their Up Leg:

Title Company:

Escrow Company:

Lender:

Loan Amount:

Interest Rate:

Amortized Over/Due In:

Notes:

#BMPB Physical Due-Diligence Checklist

Exterior
- Paint:
- Stucco:
- Siding:
- Roof:
- Stairways:
- Decks:
- Landings:
- Railing:
- Garage Doors:
- Gutters:
- Structure:
- Landscape:
- Laundry Area:
- Common Area:
- Drainage:
- Wood:
- Asphalt:
- Fences:

Interior
- Carpet/Flooring:
- Paint:
- Appliances:

- Fixtures:
- Wall/Ceilings:
- Plumbing:
- Other:

#BMPB What to Do Once You Own

1. Ensure adequate insurance coverage is in place, likely a requirement by your lender prior to closing escrow.

2. Join your local apartment association to obtain the correct forms for your area.

3. Notify tenants of change in ownership/management and provide them with appropriate contact information.

4. Clean up any incorrect or inaccurate paperwork prepared by the previous ownership or management group.

5. Market and lease your vacant apartment homes at market rate and increase your existing residents' rents to a comfortable spot slightly beneath market rate (an incentive to your loyal customers).

6. Invest in on-going maintenance, preventative mainte-nance and continual upkeep.

7. Continuously evaluate your property and look for ways to add, create or improve value.

8. Monitor the debt markets to identify when it could be to your benefit to refinance or reposition the debt on your property.

#BMPB Acquisition Spreadsheet & Rental Survey

Due to formatting issues, you must email a copy of your receipt to **info@bmbp-book.com** in order to receive your underwriting and rental survey spreadsheet.

follow the conversation on Facebook, Twitter
and Instagram by tracking the hashtag:
#BMPB

www.ingramcontent.com/pod-product-compliance
Lightning Source LLC
Chambersburg PA
CBHW071727200326

41519CB00021BC/6602